SANTA FE
FLAVORS

SANTA FE
FLAVORS
BEST RESTAURANTS AND RECIPES

ANNE HILLERMAN

PHOTOGRAPHS BY DON STREL

GIBBS SMITH
TO ENRICH AND INSPIRE HUMANKIND
Salt Lake City | Charleston | Santa Fe | Santa Barbara

To Don, my favorite dining companion

First Edition
13 12 11 10 09   5 4 3 2 1

Text © 2009 Anne Hillerman
Photographs © 2009 Don Strel

Published by
Gibbs Smith
P.O. Box 667
Layton, Utah 84041

1.800.835.4993 orders
www.gibbs-smith.com

Designed and produced by mGraphicDesign / Maralee Nelson
Printed and bound in China
Gibbs Smith books are printed on either recycled, 100% post-consumer waste, or FSC-certified papers.

Library of Congress Cataloging-in-Publication Data

Hillerman, Anne, 1949-
  Santa Fe flavors : best restaurants and recipes / Anne Hillerman ; photographs by Don Strel. -- 1st ed.
     p. cm.
  ISBN-13: 978-1-4236-0318-4
  ISBN-10: 1-4236-0318-4
  1. Restaurants--New Mexico--Santa Fe--Guidebooks. 2. Cookery, American--Southwestern style. 3. Cookery. I. Title.
  TX907.3.N62S26 2009
  647.95789'56--dc22
                         2008025261

Contents

Acknowledgments

I deeply appreciate the generosity of all the chefs and restaurant owners who made this book possible.

I'd like to thank Ellen Kleiner for getting the project underway, and Don Strel, Brandon Strel and Cindy Bellinger for their valuable suggestions on the manuscript. Winifred Rusk helped me round up the stragglers. I'm ever appreciative of my grandmothers, Margaret and Lucy, who understood the importance of a good meal.

Most of all, heartfelt gratitude to my fabulous mother, Marie, who taught me two of life's most important skills: how to read and how to cook.

Introduction
Eating Your Way through Santa Fe

Santa Fe is a fabulous town for food. Last time I checked, the city offered more than two hundred restaurants from mom-and-pop diners to elegant gourmet establishments.

As a restaurant critic for the *Albuquerque Journal's Journal Santa Fe* since 2001, I've had an opportunity to eat my way through much of northern New Mexico. I've enjoyed some wonderful meals and suffered through some dismal ones. I wrote this book to help people avoid dining disasters. In my line of work, I expect the best food and service in an atmosphere that makes dining out a pleasure—and so should you.

Some of us lucky enough to live in Santa Fe have the benefit of asking our friends where they like to eat, if they have tried the newest place, or if they've sampled a seasonal menu. Since visitors (and some locals) lack these friendly, informed connections, the goal of this book is to help you find memorable meals.

There were dozens of excellent restaurants from which to choose as I made my selections for this guide. In many cases, the decision was agonizingly difficult. The book offers a wide range of restaurants, from beloved establishments that have been open for decades to relatively new eateries. You'll find some of these places consistently mentioned in national travel guides touting Santa Fe's culinary charms. Others appeal to my sense of whimsy or my affection for small, owner-chef establishments. I've included gourmet 4-star restaurants that offer distinctive City Different ambiance, and local hangouts with generous servings, family-pleasing prices and maybe even a TV for watching the big game, even out of town.

The book includes spots for first-rate steaks, fine breakfasts and all-American comfort food. Some reflect modern Santa Fe's sophistication with their combinations of global flavors and international dining influences. In other restaurants, you might find dishes new to you, what we fondly call "New Mexican" food. Menu choices like *posole* and blue corn enchiladas have deep roots in Northern New Mexico's history as a Spanish settlement surrounded by Indian Pueblos.

The question I'm asked most often as a restaurant reviewer, and have the most difficulty answering, is which place is my personal favorite. Usually, it's the last restaurant where I ate a great meal. I would take my friends to any of these restaurants. That's why I'm sharing them with you. I've done my best to give you accurate information, but life is about change. Restaurants can move to different locations, switch chefs and change focus. If dining at one of the places mentioned is especially important to you, please double check before you plan your evening, or your vacation, around that meal.

Each chef selected the recipe that is included here with no prompting from me. Every restaurant I have included participated by invitation. No one paid to be included. I appreciate the generosity of these great restaurants in sharing their recipes. At my request, the chefs reduced the amount of food their recipes normally make to suit the needs of home cooks. Since Santa Fe sits at 7,000 feet, you'll need to tinker with the baking recipes if you live closer to sea level, and we have included simple instructions to do that.

Enjoy!

How to Use This Book

Our Price Guide

$ Inexpensive; Most entrées under $10

$$ Moderate; Most entrées under $20

$$$ Expensive; Most entrées under $30

$$$$ Very expensive; Most entrées over $30

Insiders' Tips for Dining Out in Santa Fe

- Call ahead for reservations, especially from Memorial Day through Labor Day and during the holidays. Even if reservations aren't accepted, you'll get a sense of the waiting time.
- No restaurant in Northern New Mexico requires men to wear ties, and you'll stand out from the crowd in some places if you do. But don't be shy about dressing up for dinner at a 4-star place.
- Some restaurants serve only beer and wine. Some have full bars. Some have no alcohol. If this matters to you, call ahead.
- Many of the restaurants included have lovely patios. If you plan to dine outside but get cold easily, bring a wrap even at the peak of summer. The air is thin at 7,000 feet and cools off quickly once the sun sets.
- The altitude also means that food and drink grow cold more quickly here. If you come from the flatlands, you'll notice that a glass of wine or other alcoholic libation will go to your head faster.
- Because Santa Fe sits in the high desert, restaurants are conscious of wise water use. In most places you'll be asked if you want water, and in some of the more casual spots, you may have to ask for it. Don't be offended.
- Santa Fe is an expensive town for waiters and bussers to live in—be generous to your servers.

Any resident worth her posole will tell you that traditional Northern New Mexican restaurants make Santa Fe a special place to eat. These establishments serve simple, delicious fare that combines both Native American and Hispanic traditions. (New Mexican food is different than Mexican cuisine. Mexican food will often include tasty seafood and the tart citrus flavors of limes and tomatillos.) Try blue corn tortillas, posole, *chicos* and local lamb. We locals crave this as our comfort food.

About Traditional New Mexico Food

The following list includes some items you might find on the menu:

- *Blue corn* isn't spoiled—it's fabulous and, some say, healthier for you than the traditional yellow corn. You'll find it used for tortillas. If the slightly nuttier taste appeals to you, you can buy fresh blue corn tortillas and blue corn tortilla chips in Northern New Mexico groceries.
- *Calabacitas*, a stew of squash, corn and green chile, makes a great side dish.
- *Carne adovada*, often the hottest dish on the menu, is pork permeated with a red chile and oregano marinade. Restaurants usually serve the cooked meat as a main course, a side dish or as a burrito.
- Northern New Mexican *chicharones* are crisp little bits of pork, sometimes served as a side dish or the filling in a burrito. They differ from the puffy, chip-like treats you find in Texas.
- *Chile* (we spell it with an "e" here) refers to both the sauce and the vegetable. Green chile is the fresh pepper, served chopped as a sauce or stuffed as a *relleno*. Red chile is the same pepper allowed to dry and usually ground into a powder that becomes the foundation for sauce. The color has nothing to do with the heat—ask your server which is spicier, or request a sample if you are nervous. Locals often use sour cream to temper too-hot chile. If you order a bowl of chile at a traditional New Mexican restaurant, you'll probably be asked if you want pinto beans, meat or posole in the bowl with the sauce.
- *Piñon nuts* are buttery delicious additions to salads, baked goods and sauces. In years with a good harvest you'll find them for sale along Northern New Mexico roadsides. I like them roasted.
- *Posole* refers both to the dried corn treated with lime or lye to make it more digestible, and to a stew made from the corn. Traditional recipes use pork, onion and oregano and serve red chile sauce on the side to be added at your discretion. You'll often see posole as a side dish, along with pinto beans (*frijoles*).
- *Sopaipillas*, cousins to Native American fry bread, are usually pillowlike rectangles of yeast dough. The best are light and puffy, crisp on the outside and hollow within. You'll find them both as entrées stuffed with beans, ground beef or chicken and smothered with chile, or served as bread with a traditional meal. Eat like a local and use a sopaipilla to sop up the last of the red or green chile sauce. Or bite off a corner and squeeze in a touch of honey.

Cooking at 7,000 Feet

This book presents all the recipes as the chefs prepare them here in Northern New Mexico at an elevation of 7,000 feet. If you are cooking at lower altitudes, you may need to make some adjustments. In general, high-altitude cooking involves slightly higher heat, more liquid and longer cooking times than at sea level.

Here are some tips:

- Meat and vegetables cooked on the stovetop with moisture will require more cooking time at high elevation. However, oven roasting times and temperatures are not affected by altitude.
- It takes longer to hard-boil an egg at 7,000 feet. If you start with a pan of cold water, allow about 25 minutes for an egg to be hard cooked in the shell. The traditional 3-minute soft-boiled egg takes 5 or 6 minutes in Santa Fe.
- Baking cakes at high altitude can be a challenge. Our recipes include slightly less flour, sugar and baking powder and/or slightly more liquid than a cook would use at sea level. Sometimes an additional egg may be added to provide more moisture. The oven temperature will also be about 25 degrees hotter than at sea level.
- If you're making bread in Santa Fe, remember that your dough may rise more quickly. Some cooks reduce the amount of yeast they use or add less flour to keep the bread from being dry.

Amaya at Hotel Santa Fe

I love Amaya's gorgeous patio, one of Santa Fe's most beautiful dining venues and a fine place for a summer lunch or dinner surrounded by gorgeous landscaping and stunning sculptures. Hotel Santa Fe is owned by the people of Picuris Pueblo, and you may find Native American influences on the menu. Perhaps a Native flute player will entertain in the lobby or you'll discover a lecture on some aspect of Native American history, art or culture. While you are here, notice the wonderful artwork throughout the property and in the hotel gift shop.

Amaya at Hotel Santa Fe
1501 Paseo de Peralta, Santa Fe
(505) 982-1200
www.hotelsantafe.com

Average price range: $$$
Type of cuisine: Southwest
Signature dish: Seared Moulard Duck Breast

Seared Moulard Duck Breast

Chef: Patrick Kline

4 Moulard duck breasts
2 cups olive oil
3 tablespoons whole grain mustard
1 tablespoon dry green peppercorns
$1/2$ cup fresh orange juice

4 Yukon gold potatoes, peeled and thinly sliced
$1/2$ cup thinly sliced fennel
2 cups heavy cream
$1/4$ cup grated Parmesan cheese

Marinate duck overnight with oil, mustard, peppercorns and orange juice. Place a layer of thinly sliced potatoes, fennel and a drizzle of cream on top in a baking pan; repeat layers until all ingredients are used. Top with Parmesan cheese and then cover with foil and bake at 350 degrees F about 25 to 30 minutes, until potatoes are fully cooked. Uncover and bake until golden brown. Let rest; then cut and serve. While potatoes are browning, sear duck breast skin down until golden brown. Place in oven at 375 degrees F until cooked, about 20 minutes. It should be medium rare. Serve duck on top of potatoes.

Servings: 4

La Boca

The large tapas menu at this sophisticated little restaurant changes often and includes a wonderful variety of fresh, interesting and unusual options. If you want a full meal, you can also get a more traditional, Spanish-inspired dinner. Lamb, fish, paella and couscous stand out among the choices. The bar offers an interesting assortment of Spanish wines. This spot, popular with residents and visitors, can get busy and noisy, especially on weekends. Reservations are a good idea.

La Boca
72 West Marcy Street, Santa Fe
(505) 982-3433
www.labocasantafe.com

Average price range: $$$
Type of cuisine: Spanish tapas, Mediterranean
Signature dish: Crab-Stuffed Cannelloni with Manchego Cream

Grilled Lamb Chops with Chile-Mint Agridulce

Chef: James Campbell Caruso

4–6 lamb chops
Olive oil
Coarse salt

Freshly ground black pepper
Chile-Mint Agridulce (recipe follows)

Preheat a charcoal or gas grill to medium-high. Lightly coat lamb chops with oil and grill about 5 minutes per side, or until meat is cooked as preferred. Remove the meat from the grill when the interior reaches 130 degrees F for rare or 140 degrees F for medium rare. (Use a thermometer to be sure.) Add salt and pepper to taste. Servings: 4–6

Chile-Mint Agridulce

$1/2$ cup lemon juice
$1/2$ cup honey
$1/4$ cup chopped mint

3 tablespoons chile pequín flakes
1 teaspoon minced garlic

In a small bowl, combine all ingredients. Serve with lamb chops or other meat or fish as desired. Makes: 1 cup

Cowgirl Bar and Grill

A hit with locals and visitors alike, the Cowgirl offers lunch, dinner and weekend brunch. There's a shaded patio for summer meals and a safe play area for kids. I like their tasty barbeque, big fresh salads, fish tacos and plenty of other choices. Be sure to read about the specials. At night, the place becomes a hoppin' roadhouse bar scene with live music. For the little buckaroos, be sure to give the famous "ice cream baked potato" a try. This food is fun.

Cowgirl Bar and Grill
319 South Guadalupe, Santa Fe
(505) 982-2565
www.cowgirlsantafe.com

Average price range: $$
Type of cuisine: Barbeque, American comfort food and contemporary
Signature dishes: Mesquite-smoked barbeque baby back pork ribs, buffalo and game burgers, Ice Cream Baked Potato

Main Dishes

Seared Scallops with Potatoes, Pesto Butter Sauce and Arugula Salad

Chive Sun-Dried Tomato Potatoes

2 pounds potatoes, quartered
1 cup chives
1 cup oil

Salt to taste
1/4 cup julienned sun-dried tomatoes

Pesto Butter Sauce

1/2 cup white wine
1/2 cup heavy cream
1/2 pound unsalted butter, cold

1 cup pesto (homemade or store bought)
Salt and pepper to taste

Arugula Salad

1/2 pound arugula
1 leek, diced and fried
1 tomato, diced

1/4 cup lemon vinaigrette, store-bought or
   use your own recipe
2 pounds scallops

To make the potatoes, boil the potatoes until soft. Purée chives with oil and add salt. Mash potatoes with the chive-oil mixture and stir in sun-dried tomatoes.

To make the pesto sauce, reduce white wine by half. Add cream and reduce by half again. Stir in cubes of cold butter. Add pesto. Add salt and pepper to taste. Keep warm.

To make the salad, mix arugula with fried leek, tomato and lemon vinaigrette.

To serve, sear scallops. Place mashed potatoes in the center of plate. Encircle potatoes with sauce. Place seared scallops on top. Drizzle pesto sauce over scallops. Place arugula salad atop potatoes and serve. Servings: 6

Coyote Cafe

This upscale, upstairs restaurant helped put Santa Fe on the culinary map, and it is still a treasure. There's much to be said for experience, both in the kitchen and among the servers. The food is creative and original, marked with skillful Southwestern touches. You'll probably need reservations, especially if you want to eat here during the Santa Fe Opera season or over a holiday. For a spontaneous meal, or a drink and a snack in the summer, try the open–air Coyote Cantina right next door. You can catch a glimpse of the sunset from the café terrace, and the more casual food is good and less expensive.

Coyote Cafe
132 West Water Street, Santa Fe
(505) 983-1615
www.coyotecafe.com

Average price range: $$$ ($$ at the cantina)
Type of cuisine: Southwestern fine dining
Signature dish: 24-ounce Cowboy, a house-aged steak

Chipotle Shrimp with Corn Cakes

Chefs: Mark Miller and Ben Hargett

1 1/2 pounds medium shrimp
3 tablespoons butter
1 cup butter, softened
1 1/2 tablespoons canned chipotle chiles, puréed

1 1/2 dozen Corn Cakes (recipe below)
2 green onions, chopped
1 cup pico de gallo

Peel the shrimp. On a griddle or in a frying pan, cook the shrimp in 3 tablespoons butter over low heat about 5 minutes, turning once. Roughly purée together the softened butter and 1 1/2 tablespoons chipotle purée; set aside at room temperature. Serve 3 corn cakes on each plate. Place 5 shrimp on top of the cakes and spread the chipotle butter liberally over the shrimp. Sprinkle the green onions over the top. Serve with pico de gallo on the side. Servings: 6–8

Corn Cakes

3/4 cup all-purpose flour
1/2 cup coarse cornmeal
1/2 teaspoon baking powder
1/2 teaspoon baking soda

1 teaspoon salt
1 teaspoon sugar
1 1/4 cups buttermilk
2 tablespoons melted butter

1 egg, beaten
1 cup fresh corn, divided
2 green onions, chopped

Place the dry ingredients in a bowl and mix together. In a large bowl, whisk the buttermilk and butter together, and then whisk in the egg. Gradually add the dry ingredients to the liquid and whisk until thoroughly blended. Purée 1/2 cup corn and then fold it into the batter along with the remaining corn and green onions. Add a little buttermilk, if necessary, to thin the mixture. Using a nonstick pan over medium heat, ladle the batter to form 3-inch cakes. Cook until golden brown (about 2 1/2 minutes on each side). Makes: About 18–20 corn cakes

Harry's Roadhouse

Harry's is a neighborhood place with good food, tasty margaritas, and a laid–back attitude. The menu includes comfort food and some fancy stuff, all freshly prepared and served in generous helpings. You'll find daily specials posted on the blackboard along with the day's desserts. The pies are worth saving room for—I especially love the lemon meringue. Harry's has a lovely patio garden complete with a tiny stream. It's wise to make reservations if you're with a group of six or more. During peak hours, expect to wait for a table and perhaps hunt for a parking spot.

Harry's Roadhouse
96 Old Las Vegas Highway Suite B, Santa Fe
(505) 989-4629 (Reservations only for parties of six or more)

Average price range: $ breakfast, $$ lunch and dinner
Type of cuisine: Down-home American with global influences
Signature dishes: Turkey meatloaf, Blueberry Buckwheat Pancakes with Homemade Turkey Sausage, Morrocan Butternut Squash Stew with Charmoula and Harrisa

Basque-Style Lamb Hash

Chef: Harry Shapiro

3 cups small red potatoes
3 cups premade Spanish- or Mexican-style lamb
   sausage (or see recipe below)
$1/4$ cup vegetable oil, divided
$1/2$ cup diced onion

$3/4$ cup diced mixed green and red bell pepper
$1/2$ cup chopped green chile
Salt and pepper to taste
8 eggs for poaching
$1/2$ cup crumbled feta cheese

Boil potatoes and cool, and then cut into wedges. In a cast-iron skillet, cook sausage, adding a little of the vegetable oil if needed. As the sausage cooks, crush into small pieces with the back of a wooden spoon or a potato masher. Remove the cooked sausage and set aside. Add a little more oil to the skillet and cook the onion and bell peppers together. Do not overcook them; they should have some crunch. Add remaining oil, and then potatoes, cooking until they start to brown. Add sausage, green chile and salt and pepper to taste.

Poach eggs. Put eggs on top of the hash and finish with feta cheese to taste. Servings: 4

Lamb Sausage

$3/4$ teaspoon cumin seed
$3/4$ teaspoon anise
$3/4$ teaspoon caraway
2 cloves garlic, crushed
$1^{1}/2$ tablespoons salt

$3/4$ teaspoon pepper
$3/4$ teaspoon paprika
1 tablespoon olive oil
1 pound ground lamb

Toast seeds and mix all ingredients with ground lamb. For best results, make lamb sausage the night before.

Jinja Bar & Bistro

Jinja is a neighborhood restaurant serving a popular assortment of Asian food and tropical drinks—even those exotic, old-fashioned kinds that arrive at the table on fire. The restaurant's ambiance is both intimate and elegant, the décor highlighted with replicas of vintage Asian travel posters from the 1930s and '40s. The menu features dishes from Japan, China, Thailand, Vietnam, Malaysia and Singapore, and offers both "small plates" and full entrées. I especially enjoy the Imperial Lettuce Wraps as a light lunch or a shared appetizer.

Jinja Bar & Bistro
510 North Guadalupe, Santa Fe
(505) 982-4321
www.jinjabistro.com

Average price range: $$
Type of cuisine: Pan-Asian
Signature dishes: Malay Coconut Soup, Tiger Prawn and Papaya Salad, Vietnamese Shaking Beef

Chef's note about this recipe: *Asian ingredients can be found at Asian specialty stores. You may substitute tofu, grilled or fried, for the shrimp, but the recipe will not be totally vegetarian unless you can find vegetarian versions of the curry paste and fish sauce.*

Main Dishes

Jungle Green Curry with Shrimp

Chef: Lesley Allin

Green Curry Sauce

1 tablespoon vegetable oil
1–2 tablespoons green curry paste (Mai Ploy brand is excellent)
¼ cup fish sauce
¼ cup loosely packed palm sugar or brown sugar

½ cup plus 1 tablespoon coconut cream
2 ¾ cups coconut milk
2 Kaffir lime leaves
1 tablespoon Galangal or fresh gingerroot, minced

Shrimp

1–2 tablespoons vegetable oil
32 whole Black tiger shrimp (size 26/30), deveined and cleaned, tails removed
1 cup julienned carrots
1 cup julienned eggplant (skin removed)
1 cup sugar snap or snow peas

1 cup green beans, cut into bite-size pieces
1 cup julienned red pepper
1 teaspoon minced garlic
4 cups Green Curry Sauce
4 cups steamed jasmine rice
Cilantro for garnish

To make the sauce, put oil into a saucepan that will hold at least 2 quarts and add the curry paste. Stir over low heat for 2 to 4 minutes (this "activates" the spice in the curry paste). Add the rest of the sauce ingredients and bring to a boil. Simmer 10 minutes and cool. Strain the sauce. (This makes 4 cups sauce, which is enough for 4 portions.)

Heat oil in a wok and add shrimp; stir-fry until no longer translucent. Add the vegetables and stir-fry until the vegetables soften. Add the garlic and curry sauce; simmer 1 to 2 minutes. Serve with rice and garnish with cilantro. This recipe provides for enough sauce to enjoy with the rice. Servings: 4

Mariscos Costa Azul

Mexican–style seafood is relatively new to Santa Fe, and we're fortunate to have several good places where you can enjoy it. At this friendly, colorful restaurant, you'll find delicious fresh fish, shrimp and even oysters when the season allows, all served with a smile. They have a special menu for children. If you like, you can get a cold beer to go with your dinner. This is one of my favorite spots when I get a yearning for la playa. *If only it had an ocean breeze . . .*

Mariscos Costa Azul
2875 Cerrillos Road, Santa Fe
(505) 473-4594

Average price range: $$
Type of cuisine: Mexican-style seafood
Signature dishes: Shrimp Veracruz, shrimp with butter and garlic, seafood soup, Red Snapper with Chipotle Sauce

Shrimp Veracruz

Chef: Noe Soriano

¼ cup olive oil
24 medium shrimp, peeled with tail left on
¼ cup diced red bell pepper
¼ cup diced yellow bell pepper
¼ cup diced green bell pepper
2 tablespoons chopped garlic

¼ cup sliced tomato
1 tablespoon chopped cilantro
¼ cup sliced white onion
¾ cup Clamato tomato juice cocktail
¾ cup V-8 juice
1 cube Knorr tomato base

Warm oil in a large frying pan over medium heat. Add the shrimp, bell peppers, garlic, tomato, cilantro and onion and sauté 5 minutes. In a medium bowl, mix together the juices and tomato base. Pour juice mixture over shrimp and vegetables and simmer 8–10 minutes over medium heat. Remove from the stove and serve with white rice and saltine crackers.

Servings: 2

El Meson & ¡Chispa! Tapas Bar

El Meson offers its customers a difficult decision—a wonderful Spanish dinner in the dining room, or a meal of tapas and dessert in the bar. The fresh, creative food, friendly and professional wait staff and cozy atmosphere make this one of my favorite spots. The tapas menu offers more than forty choices. If you want something different, the paella is first rate. I also like the live entertainment, including Flamenco dancing, which seems to go well with the house sangria, created with a splash of brandy.

El Meson & ¡Chispa! Tapas Bar
213 Washington Avenue, Santa Fe
(505) 983-6756
www.elmeson-santafe.com

Average price range: $$$
Type of cuisine: Authentic foods of Spain
Signature dishes: Paella a la Valenciana and tapas

Chef's note about this recipe: *A great springtime tapa treat, this dish goes great with chilled dry sherry or dry white wine.*

Steamed Clams with Baby Artichokes

Chef: David Huertas

16 baby artichokes
2 lemons, juiced
$1/2$ teaspoon salt
$1^1/2$ tablespoons extra virgin olive oil
2 medium cloves garlic, minced

2 teaspoons flour
1 cup dry white wine
24 fresh clams, cleaned
1 tablespoon chopped flat-leaf parsley

Trim tough outer leaves off artichokes and peel the outside of the stalk. Place in a pot and cover with cold water. Add lemon juice and salt. Bring to a boil, and then reduce heat and simmer 20 minutes. Strain, saving about $3/4$ cup of the cooking liquid. Cut artichokes in half. In a pan, heat the olive oil and lightly brown the garlic. Add flour and quickly incorporate with the oil and garlic. Add wine and the reserved liquid from the artichokes. Add the clams and simmer until they all open. (Discard any that don't open.) Add the artichokes and parsley and serve. Servings: 4 as an appetizer or tapa

Mucho Gusto Authentic Mexican Food

Located downtown but a little off the beaten trail, this perky restaurant draws a great local following for both lunch and dinner. It's a fine spot for families, spotlessly clean but comfortably casual. I love their stuffed chicken breast—it looks like a miniature football and the taste is sublime. The fresh authentic Mexican food they serve hails from Chihuahua. The tomatillo salsa, complete with the punch of fresh lime juice, stirs up my fond memories of Mexico.

Mucho Gusto Authentic Mexican Food
839 Paseo De Peralta, Santa Fe
(505) 955-8402

Average price range: $$
Type of cuisine: Mexican
Signature dishes: Enchilada de Mole Poblano, lamb tacos, Pollo Relleno

Chef's note about this recipe: *This sauce can be used immediately with sautéed shrimp or fish or stored in the refrigerator until needed. To store the sauce, add enough olive oil to cover the mixture completely and place in an airtight container.*

Pasilla Negro Chile Sauce

Chef: Alex Castro

½ cup (4 ounces) sun-dried tomatoes
1 red onion
¾ cup (6 ounces) whole peeled garlic
1½ cups olive oil (plus extra for soaking later)
12 dried Pasilla Negro chiles

1 teaspoon thyme
1 teaspoon tarragon
1 teaspoon oregano
1 teaspoon salt

Soak the sun-dried tomatoes in water until softened, about 15 minutes; drain. Grill the onion until blackened on all sides. Sauté the garlic in a pan with oil as needed until brown. Slice the onion and garlic just enough for easy blending. Purée the tomatoes, onion, garlic and olive oil in a blender. Grind the chiles to a powder and add to the mixture in the blender. Add the thyme, tarragon, oregano and salt. Blend again until all ingredients are thoroughly mixed. Servings: 8–10

El Nido

The ten-minute trip from downtown Santa Fe to Tesuque helps set the stage for eating at El Nido. I like to drive Bishop's Lodge Road, which winds past some beautiful homes and estates and old cottonwoods, to get to this great place. El Nido is filled with Old Santa Fe ambiance—private banco-type booths, beautiful hardwood floors and a beckoning fireplace in the front dining room. The restaurant has been serving steaks and seafood for more than fifty years. Many meals include salad and potato. Be sure to ask out about the specials—they really are special.

El Nido
1578 Bishop's Lodge Road, Tesuque
(505) 988-4340

Average price range: $$$
Type of cuisine: Choice aged beef and fresh seafood
Signature dishes: Barbeque baby back ribs, fresh steamed mussels, rack of lamb

Main Dishes

Pan Seared Pecan-Crusted Halibut
with Orange Rosemary Sauce

Chef: J. D. Damron

Sauce

1 1/2 cups fresh orange juice
1 cup dry white wine
1/4 cup white wine vinegar
8 fresh parsley stems
1 1/2 tablespoons fresh lemon juice

1 large fresh thyme sprig
2 fresh rosemary sprigs
1/2 cup cream, or to taste
3/4 cup unsalted butter, cut into 12 pieces
Salt and pepper to taste

Halibut

2 cups pecans, whole or pieces
1 cup flour, divided
2 cups panko (Japanese breadcrumbs)
2 (10-ounce) halibut fillets

Salt and pepper to taste
3 large egg whites, beaten
2 tablespoons unsalted butter

To make the sauce, combine the first six ingredients in a medium saucepan. Boil 10 minutes. Add rosemary. Boil until liquid is reduced to 1/2 cup, about 10 minutes more. Strain sauce into another medium saucepan, pressing on solids in sieve. Add cream and bring to a boil. Reduce heat to low. Whisk in butter, one piece at a time (do not boil). Season with salt and pepper. Let stand at room temperature up to 2 hours.

To make the halibut, combine pecans and 1 tablespoon flour in a food processor. Grind pecans finely and transfer to a plate. Add breadcrumbs. Place remaining flour on another plate. Sprinkle fish with salt and pepper. Dip fillets into flour to coat and shake off excess. Using pastry brush, brush both sides with egg whites. Place fillets into pecans and press to coat.

Heat butter in a large, heavy skillet over medium-high heat. Place fillets onto skillet. Cook on both sides until crust is golden and crisp, about 3 minutes on each side. Cook until just opaque in center. Transfer to plate. Spoon sauce on and around fish and serve. Servings: 2

Osteria D'Assisi

Located just a few blocks from the Plaza in a renovated historic home, the Osteria is a popular spot for a quiet meal. I enjoy summer dinners outside on the front patio, dining under the stars. The owner, who is Italian, prides himself on offering authentic Italian cuisine. The restaurant is named after the city of Santa Fe's patron saint, Saint Francis, who was born in the town of Assisi in Italy. In my opinion, the veal rolls stuffed with Swiss chard, porcini mushrooms and Parmesan cheese are especially wonderful.

Osteria D'Assisi
58 South Federal Place, Santa Fe
(505) 986-5858
www.osteriadassisi.net

Average price range: $$$
Type of cuisine: Italian
Signature dishes: Fettuccine alla Carolina, Scaloppine al Vino Blanco con Capperi

Rollatini di Melanzane (Eggplant Rolls)

Pomodoro Sauce

5 cups canned Alta Cucina tomatoes, or other
   canned Italian tomatoes
1 carrot, peeled
1 stalk celery
¼ onion, peeled

4 tablespoons pure olive oil
¼ tablespoon chopped garlic
Salt and pepper
1 small bunch fresh basil, chopped

Eggplant Rollatini

1 large eggplant
Oil for frying
Salt and pepper to taste
5 cups ricotta cheese
1 cup grated Parmesan cheese

2 eggs
1 bunch green onions, finely chopped
1 tablespoon chopped parsley
1 tablespoon chopped garlic
1 teaspoon oregano

To make the sauce, pass tomatoes through a strainer, squeezing out all the juice. Blend the remaining tomato pulp. Chop carrots, celery and onions to a fine consistency. In a large pot, heat olive oil, cook garlic to a golden brown and add chopped vegetables. Cook, stirring frequently, until all vegetables are soft, about 15 minutes. Add tomato and bring just to a boil, stirring constantly. Remove from heat. Add salt, pepper and basil. Stir and cool.

To make the Eggplant Rollatini, slice eggplant into 8 slices (setting it aside to allow for time for eggplant to discharge water), rinse and dry. Fry in oil in hot pan and then let cool. Add salt and pepper to taste. Mix the ricotta, Parmesan, eggs, green onion, parsley, garlic, oregano, salt and pepper in a bowl. Roll mixture inside eggplant slices. Place rollatini in a casserole dish and cover with Pomodoro Sauce. Cook in oven at 375 degrees F for 15 minutes and serve. Servings: 4

Pranzo Italian Grill

Known for generous portions at reasonable prices, Pranzo has won kudos for its wine selection, including local honors for best wine-by-the-glass and national Wine Spectator Awards. In addition to food, you'll find entertainment several nights each week. Don't miss the lovely upstairs piano cabaret room that looks down on the tree tops. The music goes well with pasta, pizza and even the lobster. The restaurant is in the Guadalupe Street neighborhood with parking right across the street.

Pranzo Italian Grill
540 Montezuma Avenue, Santa Fe
(505) 984-2645
www.pranzosantafe.com

Average price range: $$–$$$
Type of cuisine: Family Italian
Signature dishes: House-made ravioli stuffed with spinach and ricotta cheese, Osso Bucco, Coniglio alla Pranzo

Coniglio alla Pranzo (Rabbit with Polenta)

3 rabbits at about 4 pounds each, skinned and
   quartered
1 large yellow onion, sliced thin
1 cup extra virgin olive oil

Sauce

1 medium yellow onion, diced
3 cloves garlic, peeled and diced
2 tablespoons black pepper
1 cup dry white wine such as a Pinot Grigio

Polenta

6 tablespoons butter
1 cup finely chopped yellow onion
8 cups water, divided

$1/2$ cup fresh lemon juice
$1/4$ cup chopped fresh thyme, stems removed
$1/4$ cup chopped fresh oregano, stems removed
Salt and pepper

$1/2$ cup Dijon mustard
1 tablespoon paprika
Salt and pepper

2 cups yellow cornmeal
Salt to taste

   Preheat oven to 350 degrees F. Place rabbit pieces in a roasting pan. Add remaining ingredients and mix well until rabbit pieces are evenly coated. Roast about 3 $1/2$ hours, or until done. Remove from oven and allow to cool slightly. Pull meat off bones when cooled enough to handle and set aside.

   To make the sauce, put first 4 ingredients into a food processor. Add a small amount of water to process into a purée. Place purée into a saucepan with mustard. Cook over low heat for approximately 40 minutes. Add paprika for color and stir. Season with salt and pepper. Add the rabbit meat to the sauce and warm gently. Serve over creamy polenta.

   To make polenta, melt butter in a saucepan over medium heat. Add onion and sauté until translucent. Stir in 6 cups water and bring to a boil. Stir together 2 cups water and cornmeal. Gradually stir the cornmeal mixture into the boiling water. Reduce heat to low and cook, stirring constantly with a wooden spoon, until the mixture thickens, about 25 minutes. Sprinkle with salt to taste. Servings: 8

Ristra

If you appreciate a beautiful environment to go along with great food, Ristra should be on your "to visit" list. Come in the back door (closest to Sanbusco Center) and you have an opportunity to discover the sophisticated bar, where you can get a light meal as well as a martini. In season, the Squash Blossom Tempura is wonderful. Ristra's French owner/chef does a fine job of incorporating Southwestern flavors in his culinary creations. The Agua Fria street location is just off the beaten path and an easy walk from major downtown hotels.

Ristra
548 Agua Fria, Santa Fe
(505) 982-8608
www.ristrarestaurant.com

Average price range: $$$
Type of cuisine: French
Signature dishes: Squash Blossom Tempura, roasted rack of lamb, Black Mediterranean Mussels

Tuna Tartare

Chef: Xavier Grenet

1 ounce ahi tuna
1/2 avocado
1 teaspoon chopped shallots
1 teaspoon capers
Salt and pepper to taste

Chives to taste
Juice of 1/2 lemon
1 teaspoon chopped sweet red pepper
Olive oil to taste
1/2 ounce mizuna salad

Cut the tuna and avocado into small cubes. Put the avocado aside. In a bowl, put the tuna, shallots, capers, salt, pepper, chives, lemon juice, sweet pepper and olive oil and mix well. Using a ring mold, put the tuna in first, then place the avocado on top. Add some mizuna salad and sprinkle with olive oil. Serve immediately. Servings: 1

Santa Fe Bar and Grill

Don't let the convenient location inside a popular Santa Fe mall mislead you. This isn't a fast-food place but a real restaurant offering a nice variety of freshly made fare—salads, burgers, specials, a great vegetarian blue corn enchilada and a pleasant tortilla soup. The bar draws a congenial crowd with two big flat-screen televisions usually tuned to sports. The patio encourages guests to take a deep breath, enjoy the sunshine and be glad they are in Northern New Mexico. This is a popular place for business lunches because the prices are reasonable and the parking easy.

Santa Fe Bar and Grill
187 Paseo de Peralta (in DeVargas Center), Santa Fe
(505) 982-3033
www.santafebargrill.com

Average price range: $ lunch, $$ dinner
Type of cuisine: Southwestern
Signature dishes: Cobb salad, Prawn and Avocado Salad, daily specials

Chef's note about this recipe: *Serve with your favorite chile sauce and garnish with lettuce, tomato and sour cream.*

Beer-Battered Chile Rellenos

Beer Batter

3 eggs
2 teaspoons baking powder
¼ teaspoon cayenne or white pepper
1 teaspoon salt

2 cups dark beer
2 cups warm water
2¾ cups flour

Chiles

2 cups vegetable oil
1 pound minced, cooked chicken (boiled is best)
2 tablespoons diced red or white onion
½ cup chopped cilantro
1 cup grated jack cheese

1 cup grated cheddar cheese
½ teaspoon salt
4 large poblano chiles, roasted, peeled and deseeded
1 cup flour

Mix eggs, baking powder, pepper and salt in a large mixing bowl for approximately 2 minutes. Add beer and water and mix quickly. Add 2 cups flour, incorporating into the mix. Slowly add ¾ cup flour until the batter coats the back of a spoon. Strain the batter and set aside. Heat the oil over medium-high heat in a 4-quart saucepan. In a separate bowl, mix the chicken, onion, cilantro, cheese and salt. Slice the chiles approximately 2½ inches down the center on one side. Stuff each chile with about ⅓ cup of the chicken mixture. Roll the chile in the dry and flour then dip completely into the beer batter. Carefully place the stuffed chile into the hot oil and brown on both sides. Remove the relleno and place on a draining rack or cloth napkin to absorb any excess oil. Servings: 4

The Shed, Creative Cooking

When I first began my career as a writer, I worked downtown a few blocks from the Plaza. One of the best parts of my job was the convenience it offered to The Shed, a quick walk from my office. I love their red chile enchiladas, served flat and sizzling hot. The desserts are dandy, too. Try the mocha cake. The restaurant occupies a charming 1692 hacienda, nine linked rooms just steps from the historic Palace of the Governors. Roses and trumpet vine bloom on the enclosed patio each summer. Plan to wait a bit for lunch in the summer; summer dinner reservations are a good idea.

The Shed, Creative Cooking
113 East Palace Avenue, Santa Fe
(505) 982-9030
www.sfshed.com

Average price range: $$
Type of cuisine: Primarily New Mexican
Signature dishes: Red Chile Enchiladas, carne adovada

Chef's note about this recipe: *The pulping of pods is messy and can be done a day before making the sauce. You can freeze the pulp and the sauce. Often I will make a batch of sauce intending to use only half of it and freezing the remainder. Store pods in a dry environment. You can use a freezer if you live in a humid climate. I prefer to store all my chile products in the freezer to maintain better quality.*

Red Chile Enchiladas

Chef: Josh Carswell

Shed Red Chile Sauce

1 cup dried red chile pods
2 tablespoons vegetable shortening
3 tablespoons flour

3 teaspoons salt
2 cloves garlic

Enchiladas

12 blue or yellow corn tortillas
1 cup canola oil or shortening
$1/2$ cup minced green onion
$1^1/2$ pounds Wisconsin cheddar cheese, grated

8 cups Shed Red Chile Sauce
6 eggs, over easy (optional)
2 cups shredded lettuce (optional)

To make the red chile sauce, remove stems from pods and shake out seeds. Discard stems and seeds. In an 8-quart pot, bring 1 gallon water to boil. Add pods and cover. Boil 30 minutes, stirring to ensure all pods soften. Drain in a colander. Fill a blender two-thirds full with pods, cover with water, and pulse/blend briefly to achieve a coarse blend. After you have blended all the pods, pass them through a food mill or chinois with a trickle of water in order to strain out the skin. Yield should be approximately 2 quarts of pulp and water.

In an 8-quart pot, heat shortening over medium heat, add flour and brown, stirring constantly to avoid burning. Achieve a rich golden brown. Carefully add pod pulp to the roux (it can spit when hot) and whisk together. Blend salt and garlic in 1 cup water and add to pot. Add water as needed to achieve consistency of rich sauce, yielding roughly 2 quarts. Simmer 45 minutes to 1 hour. Stirring and a flame deflector can help avoid burning the sauce. Makes 2 quarts.

To make the enchiladas, fry tortillas in oil to soften and slightly blister. Blot oil. Place tortillas on ovenproof plates. Stack a tortilla, and cover with a little onion and cheese. Top this with another tortilla, sprinkle with more cheese and cover entire stack with one-sixth of the chile sauce. Repeat for each serving. Bake on individual plates in a preheated oven at 450 degrees F until sauce begins to bubble around edges. Serve topped with an egg and/or lettuce garnish. Servings: 6

Shohko Cafe

Don't be surprised to discover delightful Japanese food in Santa Fe. Shohko, named after the longtime owner, is Santa Fe's oldest Asian restaurant. The management and kitchen know what they're doing, as the regular customers who flock to the sushi counter will testify. I enjoy dinner in the sushi bar where I can watch the skilled chefs slice the fresh fish and prepare their creations. But don't worry if you don't fancy raw fish; the tempura is light as a cloud, and you can also order teriyaki and Kobe beef. You'll find Japanese beer and an extensive selection of premium sakes.

Shohko Cafe
321 Johnson Street, Santa Fe
(505) 982-9708

Average price range: $$$
Type of cuisine: Japanese, sushi
Signature dishes: Organic Kobe Beef Tataki, Green Chile Tempura, Santa Fe Roll

Chef's note about this recipe: *Bonito is a deep-sea fish similar to mackerel that is traditionally boiled, dried and shaved into translucent strands or flakes. These shavings are very fine and delicate. The strands are used on top of salads and cold tofu dishes, and the flakes are used in making dashi (Japanese broth). At an Asian food store they might be called "dried shaved bonito flakes."*

Green Chile Tempura and Dipping Broth

Chef: Masayuki Hattori

Dipping Broth

3 cups water
1 cup (or less) shaved bonito flakes
1 cup soy sauce

1 cup sake or sweet sake (mirin)
1 teaspoon finely grated ginger, divided
4 teaspoons finely grated Daikon radish, divided

Tempura

4 cups canola or other vegetable frying oil
6 Anaheim or Hatch New Mexico green chiles
2 cups ice-cold water
1 egg

2 cups low-gluten wheat flour (as low in gluten as possible)
¼ cup cornstarch or Japanese potato starch
¼ teaspoon salt

To make the dipping broth, pour water in a saucepan and heat on high until it boils. Add bonito flakes and turn off heat. Let sit 5 minutes, and then strain bonito from the broth. Add soy sauce and sake and return to a boil. Allow broth to boil for about 2 minutes, letting the alcohol in the sake cook away. Be careful not to over boil. Remove from heat. Place ¼ teaspoon ginger and 1 teaspoon Daikon radish each in the bottoms of four small, shallow serving bowls. Ladle warm broth into bowl. This broth can be prepared in advance and brought to soup-temperature while preparing tempura.

To make the tempura, pour oil in a fryer and allow oil to reach 350 degrees F. Slice green chiles lengthwise in half. The cap can be cut off or kept on, according to preference. Clean and deseed chile halves. Slice the halves lengthwise into quarters or maybe even eighths, depending on the girth of the chile. Put chile aside. In a large bowl, add ice-cold water. Add egg to cold water and beat. Add flour, sifting it over the bowl, and then add starch and salt. Mix batter gently with a whisk, being careful not to over blend. The batter should retain tiny clumps of unmixed flour. Batter should be runny, not sticky, but not watery. Dip green chile slices into batter, coating all surfaces. Hold bowl over the fryer to minimize batter drips and gently insert each chile strip into the hot oil. Fry for 30 seconds to 1 minute. Remove promptly. Dip tempura into the broth and eat while hot.

Servings: 4

Tomasita's Restaurant

Located in the historic Santa Fe rail yard, Tomasita's has been serving downtown Santa Fe for nearly thirty years, with three generations of family ownership. Because it's a perennial favorite among locals and visitors, weekend nights typically find Tomasita's front door surrounded by hungry people awaiting a table. You can pass the time by checking out the nearby train station, strolling the rail yard—or pull up a stool at the bar. Once you're seated, take a look at the specials. I love their carne adovada, but it's not for the faint of heart. A side of sour cream will tone down the chile's heat.

Tomasita's Restaurant
500 South Guadalupe Street, Santa Fe
(505) 983-5721

Average price range: $
Type of cuisine: Northern New Mexican
Signature dishes: Carne adovada, chile rellenos, sopaipillas

Carne Adovada with Chile Caribe

16–20 red chile pods, seeded and with stems
   removed
4 cloves garlic
1 tablespoon salt

¼ teaspoon cumin
1 tablespoon oregano
4 pounds lean pork, cubed

   Soak chile pods covered in warm water for 10 minutes to soften. Drain. Place chiles a few at a time in a blender with enough water to create desired consistency and blend until smooth. Add garlic, salt, cumin and oregano to make chile caribe, the sauce for the marinade. Place cubed pork in a baking pan and add the chile caribe. Cover and let stand for 8 to 24 hours in refrigerator. Bake at 350 degrees F for 40 to 60 minutes. Servings: 10

Andiamo! A Neighborhood Trattoria

Andiamo! (the name means "let's go" in Italian) draws a steady stream of loyal local customers to the Guadalupe Street area because of its consistently good food and the pleasant, bustling ambiance. This place is slightly off the beaten track, located in an old house converted into a cozy space for a good meal. I think their Gorgonzola sauce is fabulous, enough to make a polenta fan out of a confirmed carnivore. They do a good job with pasta, duck and fish, too.

Andiamo! A Neighborhood Trattoria
322 Garfield Street, Santa Fe
(505) 995-9595
www.andiamoonline.com

Average price range: $$
Type of cuisine: Italian
Signature dishes: Chicken Parmesan, Crispy Polenta with Gorgonzola Sauce, calamari pizza

Crispy Polenta with Gorgonzola Sauce

3 1/2 cups salted water
1 cup polenta, non-instant
1/4 cup unsalted butter
1/4 cup grated Parmesan cheese (or to taste)
1/8 cup chopped rosemary
Red wine vinegar, salt and cayenne pepper to taste

1 sprig rosemary
2 cups heavy cream
3–4 ounces Gorgonzola cheese
Black pepper and lemon juice to taste
Parsley, chives and breadcrumbs, for garnish

Bring salted water to a boil. Slowly whisk in polenta. Cook gently for about 20 minutes. Add unsalted butter, Parmesan cheese and the rosemary. Add vinegar, salt, and cayenne pepper to taste.

For the Gorgonzola Sauce, add the rosemary sprig to the cream and reduce by about half over low heat. Whisk in the Gorgonzola. Season with salt, black pepper and lemon juice to taste. Pour the Gorgonzola sauce onto a plate and spoon polenta on top. Garnish with parsley, chives and breadcrumbs. Servings: 4–8

Bobcat Bite Restaurant

With hamburgers made from fresh, natural, daily ground whole chuck, this casual little restaurant has been a local favorite for green chile cheeseburgers and fries for many decades. The name comes from generations of bobcats that visited this location in search of a handout in the days before I-25 made their cross-country ramblings more treacherous. Be prepared to wait if you come any time near the standard lunch or dinner hour—no reservations accepted.

Bobcat Bite Restaurant
420 Old Las Vegas Highway (East of Santa Fe)
(505) 983-5319
www.bobcatbite.com

Average price range: $$
Type of cuisine: American
Signature dishes: Green chile cheeseburger, steaks, pork chops

Chef's note about this recipe: *At the restaurant, we make our slaw a day in advance.*

Bonnie's Coleslaw, a.k.a. Pepperslaw/Depression Era Coleslaw

Chef: Bonnie Eckre

2–3 heads cabbage, shredded
1 green bell pepper, chopped
1–1 1/2 cups sugar
2 cups distilled white vinegar
1/2 cup canola oil

1/2 teaspoon salt
1 teaspoon pepper
1 teaspoon celery seed
2 tablespoons mustard

Place cabbage in a large bowl. Put pepper on top of cabbage. For every head of cabbage, pour 1/2 cup of sugar over entire mixture.

In a saucepan, boil vinegar, oil, salt, pepper, celery seed and mustard. When boiled, this mixture will chase you out of the kitchen. Don't breathe! Cook until mustard is dissolved, about 5 minutes. Pour over sugar, bell pepper and cabbage. When cool, mix and refrigerate. Letting it marinate will make it taste even better. Servings: 8–10

Bumble Bee's Baja Grill

Bumble Bee's serves amazingly fresh food inspired by Mexico's seafood-friendly Baja coast. In addition to fish tacos on their soft, house-made regular or whole-wheat tortillas, you can order a big variety of Mexican favorites including lamb burritos. Or try their great chile-rubbed rotisserie chicken complete with beans and rice. All lunch and dinner orders include a trip to the salsa bar while you wait. The downtown Jefferson location has a drive-through for that breakfast burrito to go, and it features live jazz on Saturday nights.

Bumble Bee's Baja Grill
Two locations:
- 301 Jefferson / (505) 820-2862
- 3777 Cerrillos Road / (505) 988-3278
www.bumblebeesbajagrill.com

Average price range: $
Type of cuisine: Mexican
Signature dishes: Tacos, breakfast burritos

Chef's note about this recipe: *If you'd like a not-so-spicy salsa, decrease the amount of serrano chiles by about half. If you like really hot salsa, add another ounce of serranos. Serve salsa with melted cheese and chicken in a quesadilla, on top of grilled meats or fish or as a snack with a big bag of chips.*

Tomatillo Salsa

Chef: Christine Galvin

1 1/4 pounds tomatillos
1/3 cup rough diced white onion
2 cloves garlic (or to taste)
1/3 cup serrano chiles

1/2 teaspoon salt
1/4 cup cilantro
1 teaspoon lime juice
1/2 cup water

Peel tomatillos and wash thoroughly. Quarter tomatillos and put them in the bowl of a food processor with onion, garlic, serranos, salt and cilantro. Purée until there are no chunks. Add lime juice and water. Purée another 3 seconds. Taste and adjust salt if necessary. Makes: Approximately 1 quart

El Farol Restaurant

El Farol introduced the Spanish concept of **tapas**—little servings of delicious food—to Santa Fe and New Mexico. Tapas choices range from marinated white Spanish anchovies to spiced quail with a sesame carrot salad and pomegranate oil. You can order hot or cold items, fancy dishes or simple plates of good cheese and fine olives. I especially love El Farol when the weather allows for dining on the portal where you can savor your food and a glass of Spanish wine. The restaurant often presents live music with local bands and draws a lively crowd of regular patrons.

El Farol Restaurant
808 Canyon Road, Santa Fe
(505) 983-9912
www.elfarolsf.com

Average price range: $$$
Type of cuisine: Spanish and classical Northern New Mexican
Signature dishes: Paella and tapas

Aguacate (Fried Avocado)

Chef: Genovevo Rivera

2 quarts vegetable oil
2 avocados
¾ cup panko (Japanese breadcrumbs)

Salt and pepper
1 cup flour
4 eggs, beaten

Heat oil in a deep pan to about 350 degrees F. Cut avocados in half, remove pits, and peel. Mix breadcrumbs, salt and pepper in a bowl. Dredge peeled avocado halves in flour, and then in eggs, and then in breadcrumb mixture. Fry until crispy and golden brown, about 1 minute. Served with cilantro, sour cream and pico de gallo. Servings: 4

The Pantry Restaurant

This long-established and much loved Santa Fe restaurant offers great lunches and breakfasts. Friendly and efficient service, good fresh food, a fair price and plenty of coffee refills are standard. The Pantry's green chile has some punch to it. I love it combined with the sour cream of the Durango omelet, smoothed into a just-spicy-enough creation. The Pantry offers daily specials well worth ordering and a happy, casual ambiance.

The Pantry Restaurant
1820 Cerrillos Road, Santa Fe
(505) 986-0022

Average price range: $
Type of cuisine: Northern New Mexican and American
Signature dishes: Fresh corned beef with red or green chile, burritos, green chile stew

Chef's note about this recipe: *If you don't want to thicken the recipe with bread or crackers, add 3 additional eggs.*

Green Chile Buffalo Meatball Appetizers

Chef: Stan Singley

1 pound fresh ground buffalo
$1/4$ pound fresh ground beef
$1/4$ pound fresh ground pork
1 cup fresh chopped green chiles
1 cup chopped celery
$1/2$ cup chopped white onion

$1/2$ cup chopped green bell pepper
3 large eggs
$1/2$ cup dried chopped bread or saltine
  cracker crumbs
Lawry's Seasoned Salt
Black pepper to taste

Combine all the ingredients, mixing by hand. After mixing, you must remove all excess air. (This can be done by slapping the ingredients several times to push the air out, or depending on the bowl, you can drop the mixture on the counter from a height of 6 to 8 inches.) Roll the ingredients into 1-ounce portions—about half the size of a golf ball—and place on a greased sheet pan. Bake at 350 degrees F for about 45 minutes. Makes: About 32 (1-ounce) meatballs

Tecolote Café

No matter what you love for breakfast, chances are you can find it at Tecolote. Folks stand in line to get into this place on weekends and holidays, and management accommodates with serve-yourself coffee while you wait. The biscuits and muffins are all made fresh in the kitchen, and the chile has a kick to it. Tecolote serves breakfast all day and offers some delicious choices for lunch. Their slogan is "No toast!" because there's no toast on the menu except the luscious French toast made with a wide variety of great breads.

Tecolote Café
1203 Cerrillos Road, Santa Fe
(505) 988-1362
www.tecolotecafe.com

Average price range: $
Type of cuisine: Northern New Mexican/breakfast
Signature dishes: Carne adovada, sautéed chicken liver, house-baked bread for French toast

Atole Piñon Hotcakes

Chef: Bill Jennison

¼ cup atole (a type of cornmeal)
1 cup sifted flour
3 teaspoons baking powder
1 tablespoon sugar
1 teaspoon salt

1 beaten egg
1 cup milk
2 tablespoons salad oil
2–3 ounces piñons, toasted in oven until golden

Combine dry ingredients. Combine egg, milk and oil, and then add to dry ingredients. Stir until moistened. (Do not over-mix; batter should be slightly lumpy.) Cook on a hot griddle. Sprinkle with piñons before turning. Enjoy with butter and your favorite syrup. Makes: About 8 (4-inch) pancakes

The Restaurant at Rancho de San Juan

For me, the lovely drive north from Santa Fe, about forty-five minutes, is the start of the fun. This small, elegant restaurant—part of a luxury inn—features a frequently changing menu of choices (usually about four entrées) with a cosmopolitan flair. I enjoy the first-rate service, fabulous sunset views and impressive wine list. You can arrive early and hike in the unusual sandstone cliffs. Reservations are essential. The restaurant and inn sit on property just across the river from one of New Mexico's first Spanish villages.

The Restaurant at Rancho de San Juan
34020 U.S. Highway 285
(Between Española and Ojo Caliente, 38 miles from Santa Fe)
(505) 753-6818
www.ranchodesanjuan.com

Average price range: $$$$
Type of cuisine: Eccentric International
Signature dishes: Grilled meats, Pacific seafood, and house-made ice creams

Rancho Deviled Eggs
with Spicy Tomato Coulis

Chef: John H. Johnson, III

6 hard-boiled eggs
1 teaspoon finely chopped jalapeños
1 teaspoon finely diced Serrano ham

1 teaspoon black truffle oil
2 fresh egg whites
Salt to taste

Tomato Coulis
1 carrot, finely diced
1 tablespoon finely diced onion
2 tablespoons finely diced celery
1 (14 1/2-ounce) can Italian plum tomatoes in sauce

1 teaspoon pimenton (smoked Spanish paprika)
1 tablespoon extra virgin olive oil
Salt to taste

Peel the hard-boiled eggs. Cut eggs in half and remove yolk. In a small bowl, mash the yolks. Add remaining ingredients except fresh egg whites and salt and mix well. Add additional truffle oil if mixture does not hold together. Stuff the 12 egg white halves with yolk mixture, making slight mounds. Beat the fresh egg whites in a bowl with salt until foamy. Roll stuffed eggs in the egg white mixture and immediately fry in very hot olive oil, turning eggs once. Eggs should have a light golden crust over them. Do not overcook or eggs will toughen. Remove and drain on paper towels.

To make the coulis, sauté fresh vegetables and pimenton in extra virgin olive oil. Add to the tomatoes and simmer until vegetables are soft and translucent. Purée and add salt to taste.

Spoon coulis on a plate and arrange egg halves over top. Sprinkle with finely chopped parsley. Serve 3 halves as an appetizer or 6 halves as a light entrée. Makes: 12 deviled eggs

Back Street Bistro

When I'm looking for a quick, reasonable and delicious lunch, this is one of my favorite choices. Away from the bustle of downtown, this restaurant draws co-workers, families and even the occasional visitor. The good smells that come from the open kitchen tell you this is the spot. You can get salads, sandwiches and desserts, as well as a variety of delicious house-made soups. The soups change with the seasons and include vegetarian options that even a meat-eater will enjoy.

Back Street Bistro
513 Camino de los Marquez, Santa Fe
(505) 982-3500

Average price range: $
Type of cuisine: American, deli style
Signature dishes: Hungarian Mushroom Soup

Garlic Soup

Chef: David Jacoby

¼ cup butter
2 medium onions
2 quarts stock (chicken or vegetable)
15–20 cloves roasted garlic

4–5 ounces grated cheddar cheese
2 cups half-and-half
Salt and white pepper to taste

Melt butter and add onions; cook until soft. Add stock and garlic. Simmer 15 minutes. Remove from stove. Add cheese and purée with hot mixture in a blender. Return to pan and add half-and-half. Finish with salt and white pepper to taste.
Servings: 8

BODY Cafe

If you've never sampled "raw food," this is the place to give it a try. Don't be scared; it tastes good! You'll find a delicious and uncooked version of Pad Thai and even raw pizza, a crust of zucchini and almonds topped with sun-dried tomato marinara sauce, olives and other treats. You can also order more traditional salads, smoothies and sandwiches. And yes, fresh hot coffee of many varieties has its place on the menu along with organic wine. The adjoining spa offers massages, yoga classes and other treats for the spirit as well as the body.

BODY Cafe
333 Cordova Road, Santa Fe
(505) 986-0362
www.bodyofsantafe.com

Average price range: $
Type of cuisine: Organic, local, primarily vegetarian, raw food and naturally sweetened desserts

Chef's note about this recipe: *When the weather starts getting warm, our bodies begin leaning more toward fresh fruits and vegetables in their raw and bursting-with-flavor state. Raw foods are not only more cooling in the summer months, but many believe this is by far the healthiest way to eat throughout the year. The theory is that when one cooks food above 112 degrees F, enzymes inherent in the food are destroyed, causing the body to expend metabolic enzymes for digestion, depleting the body's limited reserve.*

Soups and Salads

Savory Basil Raw Soup

Chef: Lorin Parrish

$1/2$ cup chopped tomato
$1/3$ cup chopped yellow onion
2 cloves garlic, minced
$1/2$ cup shredded carrot
$1/2$ cup shredded beet

1 tablespoon piñons
$3/4$ cup fresh basil leaves
2 tablespoons Bragg Liquid Aminos (or tamari)
1 tablespoon apple cider vinegar
2–3 cups water (as needed)

Combine all the ingredients in a blender or food processor and process until finely chopped but still lumpy. Pour into soup bowls and garnish with fresh basil leaves. This raw soup is fresh and vibrant, like a pesto. Servings: 4

Cafe Pasqual's

This cheerful, always busy eatery offers organic veggies, free-range poultry and naturally raised beef and pork. The owner/chef has a knack for preparing meals in intriguing and unusual ways. She is also famous for her generosity to nonprofit groups in the area. I especially love the beautiful and filling breakfast quesadillas. If you're lucky, you'll get to sit at a window table facing Water Street. The restaurant has received the James Beard America's Regional Cooking Classics Award as a "timeless, grassroots restaurant that serves memorable food and is strongly imbedded in the fabric of the community."

Cafe Pasqual's
121 Don Gaspar, Santa Fe
(505) 983-9340
www.pasquals.com

Average price range: $$ breakfast and lunch, $$$ dinner
Type of cuisine: New and old Mexican, Thai, equatorial cuisine
Signature dishes: Hand-cut corned beef hash, Huevos Rancheros, Mole Enchiladas, Wild Salmon in Banana Leaf with Thai Spices

Smoked Trout Niçoise

Chef: Katharine Kagel

Vinaigrette

²/₃ cup red wine vinegar
¹/₃ cup extra virgin olive oil
1 tablespoon Dijon mustard

¼ teaspoon coarse sea salt (or to taste)
Black pepper, freshly ground, to taste

Salad

1¹/₂ pounds Yukon gold potatoes, boiled until
   fork tender and sliced while warm
1 bag field greens or 2 heads chopped romaine
   lettuce
4 celery stalks, ends discarded and cut into chevrons
¹/₂ pound sugar snap peas, slightly steamed and
   refreshed in ice water, drained

2 large ripe tomatoes, cored and cut into 12 wedges
2 hard-boiled eggs, shelled and halved
¹/₂ pound smoked trout fillet, torn into fork-size
   pieces
24 niçoise olives, pitted
¹/₂ cup flat-leaf parsley leaves, finely minced

Whisk all vinaigrette ingredients together until emulsified, and before using each time.

Slice the fork-tender potatoes into a large bowl. Pour half the vinaigrette over the potatoes, making sure to whisk well before adding. Let cool.

On four large plates or bowls, arrange the salad by making a nest of lettuce greens, and then arrange the dressed potatoes over top. Scatter the celery and peas; then strategically place the tomatoes and egg halves for optimal color arrangement. Evenly divide the trout in large bits in the center and pour the remaining vinaigrette over everything. Add the olives and sprinkle with parsley. Serve with baguette. Servings: 4

Celebrations Village West

Celebrations started as a locals place, back when Canyon Road was a locals haunt. Established in 1987 in a former adobe home on Canyon Road, this popular restaurant moved to a less historic but more convenient location in 2007. The food is better than ever, and the restaurant now has a view of the Sangre de Cristo Mountains. I especially like the Cajun touches you'll find here, a reflection of owner Sylvia Johnson's heritage. The New Mexican food is good, too. And don't miss the tender silver-dollar pancakes at breakfast.

Celebrations Village West
1620 St. Michael's Dr.
(505) 989-8904
www.celebrationssantafe.com

Average price range: $$
Type of cuisine: Eclectic
Signature dishes: Creole Cajun Gumbo, Red Chile Piñon Brittle Ice Cream

Chef's note about this recipe: *I serve this in individual bowls with steamed rice, chopped parsley, garlic toast and a bottle of Tabasco. This recipe freezes well.*

Celebrations' Creole Cajun Gumbo

Chef: Sylvia Johnson

Roux

1 cup vegetable oil

1 cup butter

2 cups flour

Gumbo

3 cups chopped bell pepper, red, green or mixed

2 cups chopped celery

2 cups chopped yellow onion

12 cups (3 quarts) rich chicken stock

1 (28-ounce) can crushed tomatoes, drained

4 bay leaves

1 tablespoon thyme

1 tablespoon oregano

1 tablespoon basil

2 cups cut frozen okra, thawed, or canned

3 cloves garlic, chopped

3 whole chicken breasts

2 pounds Andouille or Kielbasa sausage, sliced

1 tablespoon cayenne pepper, or to taste

Salt to taste

To make the roux, heat oil and butter in a heavy pot, add flour and stir or whisk until dark brown. Stir constantly, about 20–30 minutes. Be careful not to splash this on your skin.

For the gumbo, in a pot large enough to hold two gallons, add the trinity of Louisiana cooking—bell peppers, celery and onions—with the chicken stock, canned tomato, bay leaves and herbs. Simmer on medium heat while you sauté the thawed or drained okra until the moisture is reduced. Add okra and garlic to gumbo. Roast chicken breasts until cooked and add to gumbo. Sauté sausage and add to gumbo. Add roux and simmer at least one hour, periodically skimming fat off the top. Add more broth if necessary. Season with cayenne pepper and salt to taste. Servings: 10–12 (Two gallons)

Counter Culture Cafe

Unassuming and casual, Counter Culture is a locals' favorite for good reason—delicious food at a fair price and service quick enough to get you back to work on time. You can come for coffee and dessert or a whole meal. Be sure to notice the area farm products on the menu. Servings are large and children are welcome. Ask about the specials. Counter Culture is best known for generous breakfasts and creative lunches, but they also serve dinner.

Counter Culture Cafe
930 Baca Street, Santa Fe
(505) 995-1105

Average price range: $
Type of cuisine: Cross-cultural
Signature dishes: Salmon Thai Coconut Soup, Fall Salad with Roasted Beet, Bleu Cheese, Walnuts and Greens

Chicken Tom-Yum Soup

Chef: Jason Aufrichtig

1 stalk chopped lemon grass
3 lime leaves
4 cloves garlic, peeled and chopped
3 Thai chiles, minced
2 tomatoes, chopped
2 stalks celery, chopped
1 cup chopped onion

1 cup chopped cilantro
$1/2$ cup chopped fresh basil
2 pounds cubed chicken breast
$1 1/2$ cups Thai fish sauce (or to taste)
$1/4$ cup Chimayo chile, peeled, chopped and seeded
$1/2$ pound uncooked rice noodles
$1 1/2$ gallons water

Combine everything in a stockpot. Simmer 45 minutes and serve. Servings: 10–12

Guadalupe Cafe

What better way to greet the day than with homemade muffins, a cup of tea, and eggs topped with a spicy blanket of green chile? But don't forget to try the light-as-air pancakes. And the waffles. And the other breakfast treats. The cafe—which makes all kinds of fancy coffee drinks—is also open for lunch and dinner. The pleasant patio looks out on the Old Santa Fe Trail, just across the street from the state office that provides free maps and other information for Santa Fe visitors.

Guadalupe Cafe
422 Old Santa Fe Trail, Santa Fe
(505) 982-9762

Average price range: $ breakfast and lunch, $$ dinner
Type of cuisine: New Mexican and American, including fresh baked goods daily
Signature dishes: Southwest Chicken Salad, egg rolls, Breast of Chicken Relleno

Sweet Potato Chipotle Soup

Chef: Isabelle Koomoa

4 yams, peeled and diced
1 stalk celery, diced
$1/2$ medium onion, diced
2 carrots, peeled and diced
6 cups hot water

1 tablespoon vegetarian soup base
1 canned whole chipotle chile, packed in adobo sauce
$1/2$ teaspoon cinnamon
$1/4$ cup brown sugar
Heavy cream to taste

Bring all ingredients except heavy cream to a boil. Continue at a soft boil for 45 minutes. Place all ingredients in a blender and process in batches with heavy cream to taste. Servings: 4–6

Joe's Diner

Located in a shopping plaza far from the hype of Santa Fe's downtown, this friendly restaurant reminds me of a classic old–fashioned diner. Except that the food has a real connection to Santa Fe's farmers and small businesses, reflecting a commitment to buy produce, meat and non–food items locally whenever possible. Joe's has a dedicated following that extends beyond the restaurant's south–side neighbor-hood. You'll find old–fashioned cream sodas on the menu. Don't pass on the desserts—the pie and cake are outstanding.

Joe's Diner
2801 Rodeo Road (Rodeo Plaza shopping center), Santa Fe
(505) 471-3800
www.joesdiner.us

Average price range: $$
Type of cuisine: All-American with serious roots in the farmer's market
Signature dishes: Roast duck, Crab Cakes Imperial, rack of lamb, Joe's Mesquite-Grilled Buffalo Burgers, black bean soup

Chef's note about this recipe: *This soup must be cooked 1 day before serving in order to develop its full flavor. Serve with sour cream or crème fraîche, and for garnish use chives, green onions or cilantro. Freezes well.*

Soups and Salads

Black Bean Soup

Chef: Roland Richter

⅛ cup (1 ounce) chopped garlic
¼ cup vegetable oil
1 cup diced carrots
1 cup diced celery
2 cups diced onions
1 tablespoon red Chimayo chile, freshly toasted
   and ground
1½ teaspoons cumin
1½ teaspoons coriander

2 teaspoons ground black pepper
½ teaspoon salt
28 ounces canned crushed tomatoes, lightly puréed
28 ounces canned black beans
1 tablespoon soy sauce
½ tablespoon Worcestershire sauce
½ cup red wine (Burgundy works well)
2 tablespoons red wine vinegar

Sauté the garlic in the vegetable oil until lightly browned, and then add the rest of the fresh vegetables and sauté until the onions are translucent. Add the dry spices, salt and canned vegetables and sauté 2 minutes. Next, add the soy sauce, Worcestershire sauce and wine. Gently simmer 30 minutes. Finally add the vinegar and simmer 5 minutes more. Makes: 1 gallon

Maria's New Mexican Kitchen

Maria's has established itself as a perennial favorite, keeping Santa Fe well fed for more than fifty years. Owner Al Lucero has been creating drinks long enough to actually write the book on margaritas: The Great Margarita Book. *You'll find 125 varieties of margaritas at Maria's and more than one hundred kinds of tequila to enjoy as you sample traditional Northern New Mexican cuisine. Try the green chile blue corn chicken enchiladas. (Yummm!) With its good, reasonably priced food and large main dining room, Maria's draws a crowd. Reservations are a good idea.*

Maria's New Mexican Kitchen
555 West Cordova Road, Santa Fe
(505) 983-7929
www.marias-santafe.com

Average price range: $$
Type of cuisine: Traditional New Mexican
Signature dishes: Blue corn enchiladas, green chile stew, fajitas

Chef's note about this recipe: *As with any recipe using local chile, the flavor and the piquant nature of the chile will vary. Tweak the recipe to your own taste by adding or reducing the amount of chile used. If your chile is not hot (piquant) enough, you may want to use a few canned or roasted and peeled jalapeño peppers to make it hotter. Frozen New Mexico green chile may be substituted for fresh.*

Traditional New Mexico Green Chile Stew

Chef: Candelario Gonzales

1 tablespoon shortening or cooking oil
3 cups cubed lean pork (cut into ¾-inch pieces)
4 potatoes, peeled and cubed into 1-inch pieces
4 quarts water
4 cups whole, roasted, peeled and stemmed Hatch
  green chile

3 cloves garlic, minced
1 medium yellow onion, diced
1 teaspoon salt (or to taste)
2 cups slightly crushed peeled tomatoes (canned
  stewed will work)
1 teaspoon flour

Heat shortening in a large frying pan; add pork and sauté until slightly golden, about 2 minutes. Set aside.

Rinse potatoes in cold water and then add them to 4 quarts water in a 6–8 quart saucepan or stockpot. Bring to a boil. Cook for 10 minutes, and then add chile, garlic, onion, salt and tomatoes. Lower heat to a simmer. Add flour to thicken, if desired. Continue to simmer about 30 minutes, and then add the pork and simmer at least 30 minutes more. (Best results if you simmer for 1 hour.) Serve in bowls with plenty of the broth. Servings: 8

The Pink Adobe

Founded in 1944, The Pink—as it is affectionately known by local fans—continues to offer memorable food and drink. The place had a gentle makeover in 2007 and emerged looking better than ever and still 100 percent charming. You can have lunch or dinner in the main building, the adobe home that gives the restaurant its name, or in the dining area that adjoins the bar. The Pink's signature steak combines great beef with green chile and has been on the menu for decades. I ate escargot for the first time as a child at one of these big wooden tables. That appetizer is still available here, and still delicious.

The Pink Adobe
406 Old Santa Fe Trail, Santa Fe
(505) 983-7712
www.thepinkadobe.com

Average price range: $$$
Type of cuisine: Comfort food with an upscale touch
Signature dishes: Steak Dunigan, fried chicken

Chef's note about this recipe: *Be sure to rub the herbs in your palm first to bring out their flavor.*

Lobster Salad

Lobster
$^1/_2$ **lemon**
1 bay leaf
6 cloves
$^1/_4$ **teaspoon pickling spice**

$^1/_4$ **teaspoon cayenne pepper**
Salt and pepper
1 onion, unpeeled, quartered
2 pounds lobster tails

Greens
1 head lettuce
4 stalks celery, chopped
1 green bell pepper, chopped
1 cup grated cheddar cheese
1 cup chilled cooked green beans

$^1/_4$ **cup chopped parsley**
10 pitted black ripe olives
2 fresh tomatoes
3 hard-boiled eggs, cut into wedges

Pink Adobe Seafood Dressing
1 cup mayonnaise
$^1/_8$ **teaspoon sweet basil**
1 cup chile sauce

$^1/_8$ **teaspoon tarragon**
1 teaspoon capers
$^1/_8$ **teaspoon savory (a pinch)**

To make the lobster, place ingredients except lobster in enough water to cover the lobster. Bring to a boil, and then drop in lobster. Let boil 20 minutes. Remove lobster, take meat out of shells, and let meat chill in the refrigerator.

To make the greens, while the lobster meat is chilling, take a very large platter and arrange greens. Place the outer crisp leaves of lettuce on the platter, and then break the heart of lettuce and arrange in a loose mound in the middle. Cover this with the celery, bell pepper, cheese and green beans.

To make the dressing, mix ingredients together and stir well.

To serve, place lobster meat on top of greens and cover generously with dressing. Sprinkle with parsley and place the olives judiciously on the mound. Garnish the edge of the platter with tomato and egg wedges. Servings: 6

La Plazuela at La Fonda

Eating in this beautiful dining room makes me feel like I'm on vacation in my own hometown. La Fonda hotel was built in 1922 at the end of the Old Santa Fe Trail on a site of the previous inns and in 1926 became one of the Harvey Houses, a chain of fine hotels. The interior courtyard restaurant, La Plazuela, offers diners a chance to enjoy their meals in a lovely sunlit space surrounded by hand–painted windows. The cuisine includes creative and original dishes with a Latin flair as well as traditional New Mexican favorites. Try the fresh guacamole made tableside. After dinner, there's usually live music in the bar.

La Plazuela at La Fonda
100 East San Francisco Street, Santa Fe
(505) 995-2334
www.Lafondasantafe.com

Average price range: $$$
Type of cuisine: Latino gourmet
Signature dishes: Camarrones Rellenos

Mango Gazpacho

Chef: Lane Warner

3 ¾ cups (30 ounces) diced mango, peeled and
   seeded
2 ½ cups (20 ounces) fresh orange juice
¼ cup extra virgin olive oil
¾ cup diced cucumber
⅔ cup diced roasted red pepper, seeded
⅔ cup whole green grapes
⅔ cup diced sweet onion

1 clove garlic, minced
1 serrano chile, minced
¼ cup fresh lime juice
½ teaspoon chopped fresh basil
Salt and white pepper to taste
Diced mango and sliced green grapes (optional as
   garnish)

Combine all ingredients except salt, pepper and garnish. Purée. Season with salt and pepper. You may garnish with diced mango and sliced green grapes. Servings: About 6

San Francisco Street Bar & Grill

At this second-story restaurant—a rarity in Santa Fe—you can sit by the large windows overlooking historic San Francisco Street and watch people pass by on the sidewalks beneath you. The lovely natural lighting and open floor plan speak to this room's earlier incarnation as a gallery, and you will still find art on the walls. The kitchen is open, too, offering patrons an opportunity to watch as their meals are prepared. The hamburgers are good here, and I love the salad Niçoise, complete with grilled-to-order tuna and squeaky fresh greens.

San Francisco Street Bar & Grill
50 East San Francisco Street # 2, Santa Fe
(505) 982-2044
www.sanfranbargrill.com

Average price range: $ lunch, $$ dinner
Type of cuisine: American bistro
Signature dishes: Bratwurst with sautéed onions, grilled cheese with pesto, Greek spinach salad, Mediterranean Salad Plate, New York strip steak

Peppercorn-Crusted New York Steak Salad

2 medium romaine lettuce heads
$\frac{1}{2}$ pound steamed asparagus, firm
2 fresh beefsteak tomatoes, cut in segments
1 ripe avocado, cut julienne
$\frac{1}{2}$ pound radishes, cut julienne
1 grapefruit, peeled and cut in segments
2 roasted sweet peppers, cut julienne

2 tablespoons cracked black pepper
1 tablespoon cracked coriander seed
$\frac{1}{2}$ teaspoon mild Chimayo red chile powder
$\frac{1}{2}$ teaspoon granulated garlic
$\frac{1}{4}$ teaspoon kosher salt
4 (6-ounce) lean New York strip steaks

Roasted Poblano Vinaigrette

1 medium roasted poblano pepper
1 tablespoon whole grain mustard
$\frac{3}{4}$ cup champagne vinegar
$\frac{3}{4}$ cup olive oil
$\frac{1}{2}$ teaspoon fresh tarragon

$\frac{1}{4}$ teaspoon salt
$\frac{1}{4}$ teaspoon black pepper
1 tablespoon honey
$\frac{1}{4}$ teaspoon nutmeg

Wash and pat dry romaine and cut into 1-inch strips. Arrange on plate or serving platter. Place all fruit and vegetables in diagonal layers over lettuce.

Mix pepper and spices. Lightly coat each steak in pepper/spice mixture. Grill to preferred temperature. Cut into thin $\frac{1}{4}$-inch-thick slices. Place over salad in plate center. Drizzle on Roasted Poblano Vinaigrette to taste and serve.

To make the vinaigrette, place all ingredients in a food processor or blender and purée until emulsified. Adjust seasonings to your taste. Pour over salad and serve. Servings: 4

Tia Sophia's Family Restaurant

For more than thirty years, this charming family-owned restaurant has served up some of Santa Fe's most delicious examples of traditional Northern New Mexican home cooking. I'm crazy about their breakfast burritos; they're big enough to be both breakfast and lunch. The chile is first rate, as is the service. Come back a few times and the staff will greet you by name and remember how you like your coffee. Tia's draws both locals and visitors and can be busy, especially during the summer. But the wait is worth it!

Tia Sophia's Family Restaurant
210 West San Francisco Street, Santa Fe
(505) 983-9880

Average price range: $
Type of cuisine: New Mexican
Signature dishes: Breakfast burrito, green chile stew

Chef's note about this recipe: *This green chile is simplicity itself. Feel free to play around with this recipe to get the flavor and sauciness you prefer. I've added chicken or beef stock, tried different vegetables and different spices. The only rule is that the natural flavor of the green chile must come through. You can use fresh chile if it is available.*

Green Chile Sauce/Stew

28 ounces frozen or canned chopped green chile
1 yellow onion, diced
1 potato, cubed
1 pound cubed pork or beef

1 head garlic, minced or finely diced
1 tablespoon ground oregano
Broth of your choice as needed
Salt and pepper to taste

Combine all ingredients in a pot. If using canned chile, include the liquid. If using frozen, there's no need to defrost. Simmer slowly until meat is cooked and potato is soft. Add broth to reach your own desired consistency. Servings: About 4

El Paragua Restaurant

Talk about ambiance! El Paragua, a long-established, family-owned restaurant in Española, reminds me of eating in a fun, funky museum. The place is filled with folk art, photos of famous guests, newspaper and magazine stories about the restaurant and the family that owns it. Be sure to take a look upstairs, and don't miss the tree trunk in the bar. The menu includes New Mexican favorites as well as steak and fish. Santa Fe has a sister restaurant, El Parasol, take-out only, also run by the Atencio family.

El Paragua Restaurant
603 Santa Cruz Road, Española
(505) 753-3211
www.elparagua.com

Average price range: $$
Type of cuisine: New Mexican
Signature dishes: Shredded beef tacos, enchiladas, rellenos and carnitas

Caldo Talpeno (Chicken Garbanzo Soup)

Chef: Frances T. Atencio

2 large chicken breasts, or enough to make 2 cups
   diced meat
10 cups water
1/2 cup diced onion
1 tablespoon salt
2 (10–12-ounce) cans garbanzo beans, drained

2 fresh tomatoes, diced
1/4 cup chopped fresh cilantro
1 (7-ounce) can chipotle peppers in adobo sauce,
   drained
Additional salt and pepper to taste
2 avocados, diced

Cook chicken breasts in a stockpot with water, onion and salt. Drain and reserve stock. Dice chicken and return to stock. Add garbanzo beans, tomatoes, cilantro, chipotle peppers, salt and pepper to taste. Simmer about 15 minutes over low heat. Serve hot garnished with avocado. Servings: 6

Anasazi Restaurant

The elegant food you'll find in this landmark restaurant is matched by the lovely Southwestern ambiance of the dining room and the consistently excellent service. This is the place many of us locals opt for when we have something to celebrate. The food often combines Asian and French influences with the bright flavors that have made Santa Fe a culinary oasis. In addition to the main dining room, the restaurant has two lovely small spaces for private groups and a first-rate wine cellar. As a bonus, the Santa Fe Plaza, with its shops and museums, is less than a block away.

Anasazi Restaurant
113 Washington Avenue, Santa Fe
(505) 988-3030
www.rosewoodhotels.com

Average price range: $$$–$$$$
Type of cuisine: Contemporary international with Southwestern influences
Signature dishes: Crab cakes, seafood entrées, Colorado lamb, Bittersweet Chocolate Liquid Center Cake and the Bourbon Vanilla Crème Brûlée

Chef's note about this recipe: *This dessert goes well with vanilla sauce and ice cream.*

Bittersweet Chocolate Liquid Center Cake

Chef: Martin Rios

8 ounces bittersweet chocolate
1 cup butter
6 egg yolks

4 eggs
$1/2$ cup sugar
$1/2$ cup flour

Combine the chocolate and butter in a bowl. Place on top of a double boiler and melt completely.

Place the egg yolks and eggs in a mixer with a paddle attachment. Using the paddle, whip for 2 minutes. Add sugar, with mixer still going, in two steps and then add the melted chocolate. Slowly add the flour while still whipping in the mixer bowl.

Use eight 5-ounce ramekins brushed with melted butter. Fill each about three-fourths full with the cake mixture. Bake at 370 degrees F for 6–7 minutes. Place each ramekin upside down in the center of a plate and remove the ramekin. Or present the cake in its own little dish if it is being served immediately. Servings: 8

Blue Heron at Sunrise Springs

Just a few minutes drive south of the Santa Fe Plaza, this restaurant could be a world away. I especially enjoy it in the late spring, sitting on the deck with a drink, watching dragonflies and ducks cavort on the spring-fed pond shaded by old cottonwoods. The menu changes seasonally and includes local, organic and natural products. You can hear live jazz bands outside on summer weekends. Come early and stroll the beautiful seventy-acre resort compound, which includes a Japanese teahouse, spa and arts center.

Blue Heron at Sunrise Springs
242 Los Pinos Road, Santa Fe
(505) 428-3600
www.sunrisesprings.com

Average price range: $$$
Type of cuisine: Fresh local organic with Asian influences
Signature dishes: Red chile hollandaise, house-cured salmon

Chef's note about this recipe: *Goes great with fresh strawberries.*

Basil Ice Cream

Chef: Malik Hammond

2–3 handfuls fresh basil (about 1¹/₂ cups)
2 cups boiling water
2 cups ice water
Simple syrup (¹/₄ cup sugar and ¹/₄ cup water cooked to dissolve the sugar)

4 eggs
8 egg yolks
2 cups sugar, divided
1 quart plus 1¹/₂ cups cream, divided

First make a basil purée by blanching the basil leaves in the boiling water for about 3 seconds, and then shock them in the ice water. Blend the basil to a purée with a little simple syrup just to allow it to mix. Set aside.

Whip the eggs, yolks and 1¹/₂ cups sugar until light in color. Heat 1 quart of cream and slowly blend into egg mixture; return to heat, stirring constantly until it reaches nape consistency (sticks to the bottom of spoon); cool and set aside. Whip the remaining cream with remaining sugar. Fold the cream into the cooled egg mixture and fold into the basil purée, adding to your own preference. Spin the mixture in an ice cream maker to specifications of machine. Cover and freeze before serving.

Servings: 6–8

Chocolate Maven Bakery and Cafe

In my experience, one of the most pleasurable parts of a good meal is the enticing aroma. If you come here for breakfast, you're sure to be greeted by the mouthwatering fragrance of fresh-baked goodies. Even better, you can watch the bakers in action if you sit downstairs near the bakery window. Don't miss the display case filled with temptation. The café has a broad and healthy menu, including salads that make it easier to justify dessert.

Chocolate Maven Bakery and Cafe
821 West San Mateo Road #C, Santa Fe
(505) 984-1980
www.chocolatemaven.com

Average price range: $
Type of cuisine: Contemporary American bistro
Signature dishes: Reuben sandwich, Eggs Benedict, hand-shaped pizzas

Chef's note about this recipe: *We like rum raisin ice cream with oatmeal cookies.*

Chocolate-Dipped Ice Cream Sandwich

Chef: Dharm Khalsa Segal

1 cup unsalted butter, softened
1 1/2 cups brown sugar, packed
1 1/2 cups unbleached flour
1 teaspoon salt
3/4 teaspoon baking soda
1 1/2 teaspoons baking powder
1 1/3 cups old-fashioned rolled oats

2 tablespoons heavy cream
1 egg
1 teaspoon pure vanilla extract
1 quart ice cream, homemade or store bought
1 pound good-quality dark chocolate, semi-sweet or bittersweet (if you can find couverture chocolate, use that)

Mix butter and brown sugar together until creamy and smooth. In a separate bowl, combine flour, salt, baking soda and baking powder together, and then mix gently into the sugar mixture. Mix in the oats, cream, egg and vanilla, and stir it all together to form coherent dough.

Prepare a baking tray with either baking parchment or lots of nonstick baking spray. Use an ice cream scoop to measure even scoops of dough onto the pan. Bake at 325 degrees F for 22 minutes. Remove from oven and let cool completely.

Prepare your favorite recipe for homemade ice cream or use a high-quality commercial brand. Soften the ice cream quickly by mixing with an electric mixer, or by mashing with a potato masher. The ice cream is ready when it is easy to spread, about the consistency of peanut butter. Don't let it get warm; you need to do this quickly. Spread the softened ice cream evenly with a spatula about 3/8-inch thick all over the top of one cookie. Place a second cookie on top of the ice cream, top down, and press gently together to make a sandwich. Wrap each sandwich in plastic wrap and put in the freezer immediately.

To make dipping sauce, break chocolate into bits, and then melt in a double boiler. Make sure no water gets into the chocolate, not even a drop. Remove the ice cream sandwiches from the freezer and use tongs to dip each sandwich entirely into the melted chocolate until completely coated. Place each dipped sandwich on parchment paper to set up. They are ready to eat now, or put the dipped sandwiches back into the freezer to store until serving. Servings: 4–6

Geronimo

Remarkable for both food and service, Geronimo is a Santa Fe legend. The restaurant's elegant and understated decor welcomes sophisticated diners from around the world. This popular restaurant consistently receives 4-star and 4-diamond ratings from national and international critics. The 1756 adobe home that houses the restaurant is a romantic, upscale place to enjoy a memorable meal. During the busy summer, this is one of the few spots in Santa Fe that offers valet parking.

Geronimo
724 Canyon Road, Santa Fe
(505) 982-1500
www.geronimorestaurant.com

Average price range: $$$–$$$$
Type of cuisine: Global Fusion–Southwest influenced
Signature dishes: Elk tenderloin, seared foie gras, grilled rack of lamb

Desserts and Drinks

Martini Shots—Vodka Sorbet with Caviar

Chef: Eric DiStefano

Simple Syrup
1/2 teaspoon lemon zest
2 cups sugar

1 cup water

Vodka Sorbet
1 cup premium vodka
1/2 cup peeled, seeded and puréed cucumber
1 cup simple syrup
1 cup spring water
1 teaspoon freshly squeezed lemon juice

1 cup peeled, seeded and finely shredded cucumber
1 tablespoon very finely diced sweet onion
1 cup crème fraîche
2 ounces Osetra or other caviar
8 small sprigs baby dill for garnish

To make simple syrup, combine the lemon zest, sugar and water in a saucepan. Place over medium heat and bring to a simmer. Cook 5 minutes. Remove from heat and strain into a bowl. Place over a larger bowl filled with ice water to lower the temperature quickly. Use immediately or transfer to an airtight storage container and refrigerate for up to 2 weeks.

To make sorbet, combine the vodka, cucumber purée, simple syrup, water and lemon juice in a bowl and mix well. Freeze in an ice cream maker according to the manufacturer's instructions. Place in an airtight container, cover and store in the freezer until ready to serve. Because of the high alcohol content of the sorbet, it will be a little slushy, perfect for this recipe.

To serve, place eight shallow martini glasses on a tray. Spoon a small mound of the shredded cucumber into each glass and top with a small portion of the sweet onion. With a teaspoon or small ice cream scoop, scoop out nicely rounded servings of the vodka sorbet and place one in each glass. Don't worry if it melts a bit while you are preparing the rest. Place a bit of crème fraîche on the sorbet and top that with a generous dollop of caviar. Add a sprig of dill on each and serve immediately. Servings: 8

Mission Cafe and Sweet Shop

This restaurant occupies a historic adobe home built in the 1850s and has lots of charm. The patio invites you to linger with cool lemonade over lunch. The menu, posted on the blackboard, highlights local, natural and organic meats and ingredients, and includes many New Mexican specialties. Because of its proximity to state offices, it can get crowded at peak meal times. Save room for organic ice cream, local chocolates and fabulous fruit pies from Josie's bakery.

Mission Cafe and Sweet Shop
239 East DeVargas, Santa Fe
(505) 983-3033

Average price range: $
Type of cuisine: Traditional New Mexican and American
Signature dishes: Smothered burritos, tortilla burgers, breakfast tacos, Tres Leches Cake

Julio's Carrot Cake

Chef: Julio de Lira

2 cups flour
1¼ cups sugar
1 teaspoon salt
1 teaspoon baking powder
1 teaspoon ground cinnamon

1 tablespoon vanilla extract
3 eggs
1 cup buttermilk
1 cup canola or vegetable oil

Filling

1 cup chopped pineapple
1 cup chopped mandarin oranges
2 cups shredded carrots

½ cup raisins
½ cup chopped walnuts

Frosting

16 ounces cream cheese
¼ cup heavy cream
3 cups powdered sugar

1 teaspoon lemon or lime juice
2 cups chopped walnuts

Preheat oven to 350 degrees F. Lightly grease two 9-inch cake pans with butter and flour. In a medium bowl, combine dry ingredients. In another medium bowl, beat together the wet ingredients. Combine the two mixtures and beat lightly. Stir in filling ingredients. Pour into pans and bake 45 minutes or until set. (Test for doneness by inserting a toothpick; it should come out dry.)

To make the frosting, bring cream cheese and cream to room temperature. Combine with powdered sugar and lemon or lime juice; stir until smooth. Frost cake and sprinkle with walnuts. Servings: 10–12 (two 9-inch layers)

Mu Du Noodles

This Cerrillos Road storefront looks unassuming from the outside, but don't let that fool you. The food is fabulous, especially if you're looking for authentic Asian cuisine with some original touches. The menu changes often based on the availability of local produce, organic meat and other healthy ingredients. You'll find vegetarian dishes aplenty, and the kitchen can often make adjustments if you don't want to eat meat. Nightly specials deserve your consideration. Operated by the owner/chef, the restaurant serves dinner only. Reservations are a fine idea.

Mu Du Noodles
1494 Cerrillos Road, Santa Fe
(505) 983-1411
www.mudunoodles.com

Average price range: $$
Type of cuisine: Asian Pacific
Signature dishes: Noodles, healthy appetizers and entrées, homemade desserts

Orange Blossom Custard

Chef: Mu Jing Lau

1 ¼ tablespoons unflavored gelatin
¾ cup sugar
3 eggs

2 ¼ cups heavy cream
¼ cup milk
3 cups orange juice

Mix everything except orange juice in a saucepan over medium heat, stirring constantly. Just before the mixture boils, remove from heat. Stir or whisk in the orange juice. Portion into cups for serving and refrigerate to set. Servings: 6

The Plaza Café

Not only does The Plaza Café have **the** *prime location for attracting tourists, locals enjoy the food here, too. We like sitting at a table by the big front windows watching the world walk by outside. The friendly staff is another enticement to eat at this diner, as are the fresh salads. The menu features New Mexican chile dishes, burgers and specials. The coconut pie is a knockout! The Plaza has been in business for more than one hundred years and is now in the second generation of family ownership.*

The Plaza Café
54 Lincoln Avenue, Santa Fe
(505) 982-1664
www.thefamousplazacafe.com

Average price range: $$
Type of cuisine: American and New Mexican
Signature dishes: Huevos Rancheros, chicken fried steak

Chef's note about this recipe: *You can find cajeta in Latino grocery stores or the international foods section of your local supermarket.*

Apple Pie with Cajeta

Chef: Andy Razatos

Pie Dough
½ cup shortening
½ cup butter
4 ½ cups flour

2 tablespoons sugar
2 teaspoons salt
1 cup ice water

Filling
12 Granny Smith apples, peeled and cored
2 cups brown sugar
1 tablespoon cinnamon

1 cup pecans
1 cup flour

Topping
1 egg yolk mixed with ½ cup warm water
½ cup brown sugar

1 jar cajeta, also known as Mexican caramel
   (10.9 ounces is the most common size)

To make the dough, cut shortening and butter into 1-inch cubes and place in freezer for 2 hours. Combine the flour, sugar and salt in a bowl. Add the frozen butter and shortening. Mix until mixture resembles coarse cornmeal. Add ice water and mix just until the dough comes together; the butter and the shortening should still be visible. Divide the dough into equal halves, cover with plastic wrap and refrigerate 30 minutes. When ready, roll out the dough on a lightly floured surface in a circle to about ⅛-inch thickness. Make sure pie crust is 1 inch larger than your pie pan. Repeat process for the top crust and set aside. Roll the pie crust gently around a rolling pin and unroll it over the pie pan.

To make the filling, mix filling ingredients, and then spoon into the pie pan, forming contents into a pointed mound. Use the rolling pin method to add the top layer of the crust. Press the edges of the two crusts together into a ½-inch lip standing up around the edge of the pan. Make a fluted edge by crimping the dough together.

To finish, brush top of pie with the egg wash and sprinkle handsomely with brown sugar. Cook at 350 degrees F for 90 minutes or until golden brown and juices are bubbling. To serve, cool pie completely and top with cajeta. Servings: 8–10

Rio Chama

Upscale and comfortable, the Rio Chama is known for its fine steaks, popular bar and relaxing ambiance. This gathering place for locals becomes a magnet for visiting legislators and lobbyists when the New Mexico Legislature is in session in the winter. The State Capitol, also known as the Roundhouse, is just a few steps away. In the summer, try the patios. Not a big steak eater? Order seafood, vegetarian offerings or Rio Chama's Crossroads Salad, an amazing stack of grilled chicken, roast beef, bacon and veggies.

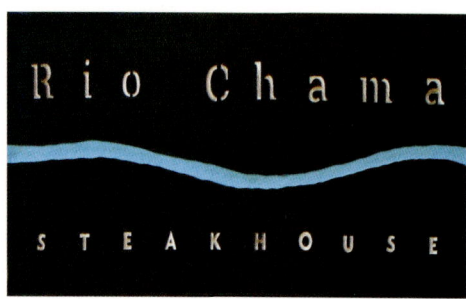

Rio Chama
414 Old Santa Fe Trail, Santa Fe
(505) 955-0765
www.riochamasteakhouse.com

Average price range: $$$–$$$$
Type of cuisine: Southwest American
Signature dish: Prime rib

Rio Chama Chocolate Pot

7 egg yolks
1 egg
$1/3$ cup sugar
$1\frac{1}{2}$ cups heavy cream
1 cup milk

2 cups semisweet chocolate, melted
2 tablespoons orange liqueur
$1\frac{1}{2}$ teaspoons vanilla extract
$1/4$ teaspoon salt

Whisk yolks, egg and sugar together. Set aside. Bring the cream and milk to a boil; whisk half into the egg mixture until smooth. Whisk the other half into the chocolate. Combine, and then add the liqueur, vanilla extract and salt. Pour into 8-ounce ramekins. Cook in a water bath at 325 degrees F for 30–35 minutes. Serve slightly warm (easily reheated) with a crème anglaise. Serves: 10–12

Steaksmith at El Gancho

A local favorite for more than three decades, the Steaksmith offers fish, vegetarian entrées, a children's menu and some of Santa Fe's best appetizers. Be sure to notice the view of city lights from the parking lot. This is the place many locals pick to celebrate birthdays and anniversaries because of the consistently good food and reliable service. You can order appetizers or a light dinner in the bar and enjoy sports on TV.

Steaksmith at El Gancho
104B Old Las Vegas Highway, Santa Fe
(505) 988-3333
www.santafesteaksmith.com

Average price range: $$$
Type of cuisine: American
Signature dishes: Spinach cheese balls, aged beef, fresh seafood, homemade desserts

Fresh Raspberry Pie with Vanilla Wafer–Almond Crust

Crust

1½ cups crushed vanilla wafers

½ cup chopped toasted almonds

¾ cup unsalted butter, melted

Glaze

1 cup raspberry purée (32 ounces frozen raspberries pressed through a strainer)

1 cup sugar

¼ cup water mixed with 5 tablespoons cornstarch, blended

A few drops almond extract

Filling

¾ cup cream cheese

1 tablespoon sugar

A few drops raspberry extract for color

A few drops almond extract

½ cup heavy cream

4 pints whole fresh raspberries

To make the crust, mix ingredients, and then press into pie pan and place in oven at 350 degrees F for about 5 minutes.

To make the glaze, combine glaze ingredients, bring to a boil and cook, stirring constantly, until translucent. Chill.

To make the filling, combine all filling ingredients except fresh raspberries. Whip together into a smooth, spreadable consistency.

Leave fresh raspberries whole. Spread a light layer of cream cheese filling over crust. Place raspberries on top and then pour glaze over berries. Fill in the spaces between berries with glaze, using a rubber spatula. Chill. Before serving, run a pie server between the crust and the pan to loosen. Serve topped with powdered sugar and sweetened fresh whipped cream.

Servings: 8–10

Trattoria Nostrani

This is a great place for splurging on a special meal. The owner, chef and staff are famous for their attention to detail. The Italian-inspired menu changes six times a year. To go with the creative approach to traditional Italian fare, the restaurant has one of Santa Fe's most extensive wine lists. From May though September, the front garden explodes with a profusion of flowers—one of downtown's nicest displays. Be sure to make a reservation if you want to eat here because seating is limited. The restaurant is serious about its "no fragrance" rule: patrons are not allowed to wear perfume or cologne.

Trattoria Nostrani
304 Johnson Street, Santa Fe
(505) 983-3800
www.trattorianostrani.com

Average price range: $$$$
Type of cuisine: Classic Northern Italian
Signature dishes: Calamari Fritti, jumbo lump blue crab risotto, Veal Milanese

Chef's note about this recipe:
Panna cotta's translation is "cooked cream." It is commonly considered an eggless custard held together with just enough gelatin. Too little gelatin and it won't hold; with too much it becomes rubbery. The final product with the right amount of gelatin should quiver.

Panna Cotta with Wafer Cookies

Chef: Nelli Maltezos

Panna Cotta
3/4 cup heavy cream
1/4 cup sour cream
2 tablespoons sugar

1/2 vanilla bean, split in half lengthwise and scraped
1/2 sheet of gelatin (available from chef's supply stores)
1/4 cup milk

Wafer Cookies
4 tablespoons butter
2 tablespoons sugar, plus more for sprinkling
1 egg yolk

1/8 teaspoon salt
1/2 cup flour, sifted with 1/8 teaspoon baking powder

To make the Panna Cotta, in a heavy-bottom saucepot place the cream, sour cream, sugar and vanilla bean. Place over low heat and warm slowly, whisking from time to time. It is crucial that the liquid never simmers and definitely never boils. You just want the sugar to dissolve completely in the hot liquid.

While the liquid is on the stove, place the gelatin sheet in a container with very cold water. Once the sugar has dissolved, remove the pot from the heat. Gently squeeze the excess water from the gelatin, and then add it to the liquid. Whisk to ensure full incorporation of the gelatin. Next add the milk and strain through a very fine mesh strainer. Divide the mix into four (3.25 ounce) molds, filling just short of the rim. Allow 3 hours for the molds to set.

To make the wafer cookies, preheat oven to 300 degrees F. Place butter and sugar in a mixer and cream. Next add the egg yolk, salt and flour/baking powder. Paddle for a few minutes until a ball forms. Wrap in plastic. Let dough rest in the refrigerator at least 30 minutes. Remove dough and unwrap. Flour a work surface and rolling pin and roll out the dough to 1/8 inch thick. Rotate dough and lightly flour it on top and bottom as you go to avoid sticking. With a cutter the same shape and diameter as the mold, cut out the wafers and place on a sheet tray lined with parchment paper. Place the wafers in oven for 25 minutes. The cookie is ready when it is still a light golden color. While the cookies are hot, sprinkle with granulated sugar and cool.

Once the panna cottas have set, run a knife along the edge of mold. Place them at a time in a very hot water bath for a few seconds. Remove and wipe dry. Place a wafer on top and turn the panna cotta upside down, holding the wafer in place. The wafer will be on bottom. Serve with fresh fruit, fruit sauce or caramel sauce. Servings: 3–4

Vanessie Santa Fe

Vanessie's specializes in entertainment and generosity. Many nights of the year, the restaurant opens it doors to Santa Fe's nonprofit arts and human services groups, hosting benefits and donating part of the proceeds to good causes. The beautiful bar room features a grand piano with a huge mirror behind it, and it hosts piano players and singers most nights of the week. The menu is steaks and seafood, with some well-priced specials that include salads and appetizers. Try their irresistible onion loaf.

Vanessie Santa Fe
434 West San Francisco Street, Santa Fe
(505) 982-9966
www.vanessiesantafe.com

Average price range: $ bar menu, $$$ dinner menu
Type of cuisine: American steaks and seafood
Signature dishes: Classic onion loaf, surf & turf, New Zealand rack of lamb, elk tenderloin

Razztini Cocktail

1 part Absolut
1 part Chambord

1 part lime juice
Lemon twist

Pour into a shaker and shake vigorously. Serve in a chilled martini glass garnished with a lemon twist. Servings: 1

La Casa Sena

This beautiful restaurant is sheltered in the landscaped courtyard of a building that belonged to one of Santa Fe's leading families. It is an unexpectedly quiet oasis location in Santa Fe's busy downtown. The building, an adobe hacienda, was built in the 1800s, restored in the 1920s and gently updated to meet code and twenty-first century expectations. You can eat beneath the ancient trees, in a formal dining area or in the lively cantina where show tunes are part of the menu. The restaurant has a wine list of more than 1,500 bottles and its own wine shop.

La Casa Sena
125 East Palace Avenue, Santa Fe
(505) 988-9232
www.lacasasena.com

Average price range: $$$ lunch, $$$$ dinner
Type of cuisine: Innovative Southwestern
Signature dishes: Cumin-Crusted Venison Tenderloin, Trout Baked in Adobe, Wrapped in Banana Leaves

Chocolate Red Chile Soup

Chef: Patrick M. Gharrity

1 quart heavy cream
11 ounces premium milk chocolate

¼ teaspoon Chimayo red chile powder
Dash salt

Heat cream to just before scalding. Add chocolate and remove from heat. Stir until chocolate is completely melted. Add chile powder and salt. Cool and serve as dessert. Servings: 4–6

Index

RESTAURANTS

RECIPES

Metric Conversion Chart

Liquid and Dry Measures

U.S.	Canadian	Australian
¼ teaspoon	1 mL	1 ml
½ teaspoon	2 mL	2 ml
1 teaspoon	5 mL	5 ml
1 tablespoon	15 mL	20 ml
¼ cup	50 mL	60 ml
⅓ cup	75 mL	80 ml
½ cup	125 mL	125 ml
⅔ cup	150 mL	170 ml
¾ cup	175 mL	190 ml
1 cup	250 mL	250 ml
1 quart	1 liter	1 litre

Temperature Conversion Chart

Fahrenheit	Celsius
250	120
275	140
300	150
325	160
350	180
375	190
400	200
425	220
450	230
475	240
500	260